COFFEE SELF-TALK FOR TEEN GIRLS

5 MINUTES A DAY FOR CONFIDENCE, ACHIEVEMENT & LIFELONG HAPPINESS

KRISTEN HELMSTETTER

Green Butterfly Press

VI.0

ABOUT THE AUTHOR

In 2018, Kristen Helmstetter sold everything to travel the world with her husband and daughter. She currently lives in a medieval hilltop town in Umbria, Italy.

You can find her on Instagram at:

instagram.com/coffeeselftalk

OTHER BOOKS BY KRISTEN HELMSTETTER

Coffee Self-Talk for Teen Girls Blank Journal (with lines)

Coffee Self-Talk: 5 Minutes a Day to Start Living Your Magical Life

The Coffee Self-Talk Daily Reader #1: Bite-Sized Nuggets of Magic to Add to Your Morning Routine

The Coffee Self-Talk Blank Journal (with lines)

Coffee Self-Talk for Dudes: 5 Minutes a Day to Start Living Your Legendary Life

The Coffee Self-Talk Guided Journal (coming 2021)

Pillow Self-Talk (coming 2021)

CONTENTS

THE KEY TO THE MAGICAL KINGDOM

The following book holds the key to the magical kingdom for the life you want.

Possibilities await. For you.

Are you ready?

INTRODUCTION

Dear Reader,

A few years ago, I did something that changed my life forever. It allowed me to attract amazing new things and people into my life, it boosted my confidence and self-esteem to crazy levels, and it catapulted my career onto a trajectory of major success. *This thing* I did, it's like a key to a magical kingdom because it has given me the opportunity to live the most magical life I could have ever imagined.

I wrote a book about *this thing* I was doing that makes my life so great, and the book sold really well.

I started to receive emails from people all over the world, telling me how it had changed their lives. And many people asked me to write a version for teens.

Hell yes, I thought. *Teens need this magic key to life, too.*

You see, I was a teenager once. You probably knew that. And although I was fairly successful at it (I graduated, went to college), I had my ups and downs. Some big ones.

But... *if I knew then what I know now*, it would've been a completely different experience. I would've glittered and shined my way through. I would've been so much happier. I would've had tons more confidence, way more success in my classes, and in my dealings with other people.

I would've started my *happily ever after* a lot earlier in life.

Because *happily ever after* is what's going on for me now. It doesn't always happen for everyone, though. Getting older is no guarantee of finding happiness. It's not like, just because you graduate high school, life gets easy and everything just falls into place. It doesn't. Not all by itself.

My happiness came because of *this thing* I do that changed my life.

In other words, what I do, *this thing* you're going to discover for yourself, that makes my life magical *now*, you can use to make *your* life magical *now*, too. And for the rest of your life.

If you're under the age of 18, you probably have other people guiding you, helping you, and making decisions for you. However, you'll see that *this thing* I've been alluding to will help you, even though you're not on your own yet, and your life is still influenced by adults.

Your parents and teachers might control some things in your life, but there's one thing that they don't control: your mind.

But I'm getting ahead of myself. More on all that exciting stuff in a bit.

First, a quick word about me. As I write this, I'm 44 years old, a (cool) mom of a daughter, I'm married to an amazing guy (we're talking *cinematic* romance), and I spend half my year in romantic Italy. I'm also a successful author, and I gotta say, never in my life did I see that coming—and I especially didn't see this back in high school. But how that happened is a magical story for later in the book.

And best of all? I'm happy, calm, smart, and glitter-shining-shimmery as *effin' hell*.

I'm going to tell you the super simple *thing* I do that makes my life amazing. That's what this book is all about. I'm going to teach you my secret, and I guarantee you'll be able to do it, because anybody can do it.

I'll tell you straight up the incredible things you can do, and that they *will* help you live your most magical life... *if you do them*. The techniques are not difficult. But they do require that you do them consistently.

I have a ton of sparkling tips and tricks up my sleeve so you can navigate life with more ease and excitement. I'll share it all. So, my dear beautiful reader, peek inside, and see which gems sparkle brightest for you.

Whatever is going on in your life right now... with school, friends, relationships, work, sports, exams, or next steps like college, or your magnificent future... this book applies to you. Now, and in the future. You can wake up every morning looking forward to your day, charging forward with passion and enthusiasm.

Let's get started!

Love,

Kristen

P.S. I am here for you, and I love hearing from readers. Reach out to me at Kristen@KristenHelmstetter.com if you have any questions, comments, or if you just want to gab.

PART I

CREATING A MAGICAL LIFE WITH COFFEE SELF-TALK

Chapter 1

THE KEY TO THE KINGDOM

OK. Are you ready?

What is *this thing* I've been gushing about? What is this key to the magical kingdom of life?

It's your self-talk.

Self-talk?

What the heck is self-talk?

Self-talk is simply the words you say or think to yourself, about yourself, your life, and the world around you. These words you say—out loud or silently—determine how you see the world. They determine your beliefs and actions. And these words have the power to attract the most amazing life, if you say the right kind of things.

Here are some examples of positive self-talk:

I am a good person.

I like today. I like my life.

I will have a good day today because I'm ready.

I make excellent grades, and only good lies before me.

I like feeling happy.

I approve of myself because I have a big heart.

I achieve because I persevere.

I choose to feel good about myself because I'm worthy.

I am pretty.

I always have a choice.

I'm healthy and happy.

I have a good attitude.

I love me just the way I am, right now.

That's self-talk. And, crazy as it may sound, it can literally change your life.

I know, you're probably thinking, *Words? That's the key to the kingdom?*

YES!

Ok, Then What Is Coffee Self-Talk?

Coffee Self-Talk is a *very special* daily ritual where you basically cast spells over your life to make it the best life ever. While drinking your cup of coffee. Or tea, milk, water, protein shake, juice, smoothie... whatever you like to drink in the morning. (From here on out, I'll always refer to the beverage as *coffee*, because I love coffee.)

Cast spells?

Sort of, yeah.

Here's what's really going on. You're drinking coffee, and instead of getting on your phone for social media stuff, you take the five minutes to drink your coffee, and you focus the time on you and your awesomeness. You say (or read, or think) special words *about you and your life*, and you make them all glittery and super positive.

So, Coffee Self-Talk just means coffee + words.

Seriously. It only takes about five minutes a day, drinking coffee and saying nice things to yourself. *But here's the kicker:* The spellcasting part... this process *transforms your life*.

How?

It makes you like yourself and your life more. It makes you believe in yourself. It helps you do whatever you set out to do, it helps you be an academic badass, a creative visionary, and it fills you with happiness. It essentially helps you create and attract *the most amazing life*.

See? Like casting a magic spell over your life.

This whole process of using your words and thoughts to change your life might be new and weird, or even sound wacky to you. But I'm living proof of how this amazing combination of words, java, and daily ritual can powerfully affect your mood, your behavior, and how you feel about yourself deep down inside. If your life is difficult right now, it will help make things better. If your life is already pretty awesome, it will still help make things better. No matter what's going on in your life right now, it'll get better.

If you're willing to have an open mind and give it a try, it might blow your mind. If you give it a solid go, your life *will* change, improve, be better, be amazing. But it's up to you to do it.

Parts I and II of this book explain everything you need to know about Coffee Self-Talk and how to do this powerful, five-minute ritual. Later, in Part IV, I provide you with scripts that tell you exactly what words to say during your morning Coffee Self-Talk. But get your glitter pens and stickers ready, because I also teach you how to write your own! You can also write them on your phone and use emojis. I do this all the time!

Timing

The ideal time to do this amazing ritual is in the morning, before you go to school. For many students, mornings are rushed. If that's you, I have a few suggestions.

Um... get up five minutes earlier? (And go to bed five minutes earlier to compensate.)

If that doesn't work, do your Coffee Self-Talk after school, but with decaf coffee, so that caffeine doesn't interfere with your sleep.

Regardless of what time you do your routine, the most important thing is doing it *every day*. Ideally, at the same time every day. By tying the activity to a specific beverage, and a specific time of day, this regular occurrence becomes a special ritual you look forward to. Once you start feeling the happiness, you will *want* to do it every day!

Your whole wonderful life lies ahead of you. No matter what path you take, there will be challenges and triumphs. My goals with this book are to:

- Show you the power you have over your own mind
- Help you reach any goal you desire
- Give you a simple way to make any tough or anxious times easier
- Teach you how to be happy no matter what's going on

The skills you'll learn in this book really can help you live your best life and make your dreams come true. Once you learn these skills, they'll always be there when you need them, for the rest of your life.

OK. Let's really begin.

Your Self-Talk Is the Most Important Thing in the World

Even if you've never heard of self-talk, you've actually been doing it your whole life. It's been around for a long time, probably since humans started talking. I'll repeat the definition of self-talk: It's the words you say and think to yourself, about yourself and the world.

It's your inner voice, your internal dialog.

Sometimes it's spoken, sometimes it's silent.

Sometimes you're aware of it, usually you're not... *until you are.*

This book will help you with becoming aware of it.

Your self-talk is the way you see yourself, refer to yourself, and think about your life. Do you think you're smart? Not smart? That's your self-talk. Do you think you're fortunate? Unfortunate? That's your self-talk. Do you think you're a good student? A poor student? That's your self-talk. Do you think you're pretty? Not pretty? Talented? Not talented? That's all self-talk.

As you can see, self-talk can be good or bad, helpful or harmful.

An *affirmation* is a statement that's said *as though it's true.* Affirmations make up your self-talk. They can be positive or negative. An affirmation can be wonderful, or it can be a mean-ass monster. Everything we say or think about ourselves, and our lives, *becomes our truth* as we say it—positively or negatively. And here's the kicker: Whether the affirmation is true or not, *your mind believes it.*

What?

Yeah. It sounds crazy, but whatever you say and think about yourself repeatedly, whether it's true or not, becomes your truth. Because of this, you actually have *a lot* of power with the words you speak and think. Your mind is like a magic wand. You say the words, you cast the spell, and the magic wand (your mind) starts to make it happen.

I know this probably sounds like BS, but it's actually not. Hang with me, and I'll explain why it's true.

The part of your brain we're talking about is your subconscious. It's the part that manages all the behaviors you do that you're not consciously aware of. And this is actually most of what goes on in your brain. The stuff you're aware of is just a small part.

The part you're aware of—such as the "you" that's reading these words right now—it judges things constantly. I like this, or I don't like that, or I believe this, or I don't believe that.

But the subconscious mind doesn't operate the same way. It just takes in data and acts on it. If it hears something enough times, it will act on it as though it's true.

Your subconscious mind *will* do what you say because that's its job. It doesn't pass judgment on the orders you give it. It just follows orders like a robot. If it's been given bad instructions, it will behave badly, leading to an unhappy life.

I'm going to teach you how to give it good instructions.

How?

With self-talk.

This is why your self-talk has the power to change your life. Many people have crappy self-talk, because they don't realize how powerful it is, and they haven't given it much thought. And they've picked up bad self-talk from others. But once they start improving their self-talk, they're shocked at how great life feels. Some people feel a difference immediately. For others, it can take a couple of weeks. But eventually, they start to speak and think differently about themselves (and the world around them), and things start to change! They're blown away by how many good things just start happening for them in their life, as if *by magic.*

But it's not magic. It's simple cause-and-effect.

The funny thing is how *simple this all is.*

But. Just because it's *simple* doesn't mean it's *easy* for everyone. That's because most people aren't used to being nice to themselves. It can feel weird at first. You might feel the urge to resist... or have difficulty even saying the words. Because they don't fit with your current self-image. But that's ok. It's totally normal and not a problem at all. That's going to change by the end of this book. You're going to become your own BFF, and when you do, the magic starts, and real transformation begins.

Caterpillar to butterfly stuff.

Self-Talk Is Used by the Best

While self-talk is ancient, it only started becoming called "self-talk" in the twentieth century. During the '70s and '80s, the term began to enter mainstream awareness, as people realized they could change their brains and behavior by changing what they say and think to themselves.

As a result, self-talk has become a mega popular tool in the personal development toolkit, particularly among high-performance people like corporate CEOs, entrepreneurs, celebrities, athletes, and elite soldiers.

So, you're in excellent company.

"Coffee Self-Talk"—that is, combining positive self-talk with a daily coffee routine—is my own customized, personal version of self-talk. It's a way of treating self-talk like it's important, focusing on it, and making it a special ritual, for just five minutes a day. (Some people do more, but five minutes will work.) And most of all, making it a ritual ensures that you do it. Every. Single. Day.

That's key.

You can miss a day now and then, but the main thing is, it's part of your normal routine. Like brushing your teeth. You wouldn't skip a day of brushing your teeth, would you? *Ew!*

Well, if your teeth are important, *so is your mind.*

Coffee Self-Talk is a combination of classic self-talk, for boosting self-esteem and adjusting your beliefs and behaviors, plus awesome affirmations. And, if you like, you can add song lyrics, quotes, passages from your favorite books, or any other words that inspire or uplift you.

And, of course, *coffee.*

When your self-esteem is boosted, you like yourself. You like your life. If you were feeling down, or not loving life before, everything changes. You become a shooting star, excited to take on the day. Heck, you're excited about your *life!* When your behaviors—and in particular, your daily habits—are in sync with your long-term goals and dreams, then things in your life seem to magically "happen" for you. Everything clicks. You start to feel like the luckiest girl alive.

Again, it feels like magic.

But it's not. It's just how the brain works. (*Pssst... but it sure feels like magic!*)

I do my Coffee Self-Talk every day, virtually without fail. I show up every morning because it inspires me, and it makes me feel so good. It helps me manifest everything I want in my life, from love, to friends, to money, to happiness. It makes every day sparkle like a diamond because I attract so many amazing things into my life... wonderful people, opportunities, health, wealth... you name it.

Your daily Coffee Self-Talk brings you closer to your goals and dream life. It can help you with all kinds of things:

- Anxiety and stress
- Fear
- Relaxing
- Confidence
- Grades

- Sports
- Creativity
- Improving any skill
- Beauty
- Finding beautiful love
- Fantastic friendships
- Fitness, weight loss, and muscle gain
- Peer pressure
- Getting stuff done and smashing goals
- Finding your passion, and
- *Making you wildly happy*

Yeah, it can do all that.

You, the Boss Lady

You are in charge of your mind. And therefore, you are in charge of your experience in life. You determine how you feel in any given moment, no matter what's going on, based on your *reactions*. This doesn't mean you won't ever have challenges... we all have challenges. Rather, it means you'll handle them much better. Life's ordinary challenges won't phase you. Or completely freak you out. It will be like in *The Matrix*, when bullets fly at Neo, and he just bends out of the way, no big deal. THAT'S how Coffee Self-Talk works for you when crap flies your way. You just bend like tall grass in the breeze.

This means it's ok when the world throws you a curve ball. You just bob-n-weave some magic, rapidly recovering. That's mastery! That's being the real hero in your life... responding better, stronger, faster, smarter. This gets you back to happiness and moving forward.

Life is supposed to be BIG fun. Your self-talk makes it so.

Fasten your seatbelt, and start your engine. Because today, you're going to start creating your new life. You're going to:

1. Decide you're worthy of an awesome life. Claim it! *This decision allows the process to start.* If you don't feel this now, don't worry. You will by the end of the book.
2. Believe it's possible. *Belief makes it happen.* Don't worry if you don't yet believe it's possible, you will by the end of the book. Just stick with it!
3. Show up and do it. Commit to yourself that you're going to do this, and then watch as strange, cool, and incredibly neat things start to happen in your life.

It's really not hard. Once you learn the basics, all you have to do is say a few words and drink a cup of delicious coffee once a day. *What could be easier?*

Are You Ready?

Of course you are, and I'm excited to be on this life-changing journey with you. Remember, I'm here for you, every step of the way. I do my Coffee Self-Talk every day, because I believe in it, because I believe in me, and guess what? I believe in *you* (because I know you're amazing, and because I know this stuff actually works). *Squeeeal! I am so eager to see this change your life.*

Here's what's going to happen in this book. Over the next few chapters (Part I), I'm going to show you why your positive self-talk is so powerful, so you can see all the benefits. This will help get you focused and excited to begin and stick with it.

I'm going to repeat some points a few times... this is intentional. It will help the concepts stick in your brain, so you'll never forget them. The repetition not only helps you learn, it keeps you motivated to continue.

After I've explained everything, I'll show you how to make your own special, daily ritual with your coffee and your self-talk so that you start every day with a bang. You'll also learn how to easily write your own powerful, fun self-talk "scripts," which you can use every day.

Later in this book, you'll find how you can use your self-talk in different parts of your life, to help you attract all the things you want and kick butt on reaching your goals. For example: friendships, family, school, self-esteem, sports, future success, beauty, and more. Each chapter in Part IV has pre-written self-talk scripts you can jump into right away and use. (Or you can write your own.)

You'll also discover tips and tricks to enhance your self-talk, turbo-charging it, as though sprinkling magic, golden pixie dust on it, speeding up the whole process.

In a Nutshell

Self-talk is the key for living a happier life, and by creating a daily Coffee Self-Talk program, you're fast-tracking your success and happiness. By using this *key to the kingdom*—this process—you're being bold, taking action, and standing up for your own incredible self. You're going after what you deserve. *The most awesome life ever.*

After you've gone through this process, you will see things (yourself, others, and the world) differently than most other people do. It's a kind of superpower, not kidding. And you know what? You're so worth it. I know you are. In fact, everyone is worth it. Imagine a world with happier teens all over the place. Adults, too. We all can live a *feel-amazing* life. We all can be *waaay* happier and not just crush our goals, but crush them with style! Pizzazz! All we need is a fun, powerful process to make it all happen.

That's what this book is for.

The greatest discovery of any generation is that a human being can alter his life by altering his attitude.

— WILLIAM JAMES

Chapter 2

CHANGE YOUR SELF-TALK, CHANGE YOUR LIFE

High school can sometimes be hard, but when you start using self-talk to your advantage, everything starts to get better. And after a few weeks, it just keeps getting better. Before you know it, you've equipped yourself with a skill that will help you for the rest of your life.

Here's What You Need to Know Right Now

All of your self-talk—the positive and negative—impacts you NOW.

The words you think and say to yourself, good or bad, *will* create that good or bad life for you. Good self-talk is the foundation of a good life. Bad self-talk is a surefire recipe for a crappy life. Because you have the power to choose your self-talk, you have the power to choose whether your life is good or bad.

It's that simple.

This is because your self-talk actually changes your brain. Human brains are *neuroplastic*, which means they can change in drastic ways, no matter how old you are. It's how we learn new skills, like playing the piano, or driving a car, or learning a new language, or in my case, learning to write fiction (romance novels) in my forties.

It also means our thought patterns can change, too, such as how we look at the world or respond to things that happen to us. When you learn new things, your brain's cells (called neurons) take action! You're the director, they're the actors. You're the general, they're the soldiers under your command. They do whatever you tell them to do. You're the coach, they're the players on the field.

This is important because it's how your Coffee Self-Talk helps you get on the right trajectory to loving your life and attracting everything your heart desires. Because you—*you!*—determine what takes root (or doesn't) inside your head, based on what you're thinking and feeling in every moment. Coffee Self-Talk gives you that control.

How Do You Know When Self-Talk Is Bad?

It's easy... bad self-talk is any word or thought about you, your life, your circumstances, or the world that isn't uplifting. If you complain or criticize anything, or anyone, that's bad self-talk. Don't like the size of your thighs? That's bad self-talk. Not happy with your car and complaining about it? That's poor self-talk. Whining about the teacher you don't like. Bad self-talk. Feel like you can't get great grades? That's really awful self-talk. Feel like you aren't good enough to deserve the love of someone wonderful? That's totally screwed-up self-talk.

You see, good self-talk is having a tornado of glittery, positive thoughts that feel good swirling around your brain and coming across your lips. You feel uplifted and energized as they spark joy when thought or uttered. When you congratulate yourself on a good job, or you think you look pretty no matter what, or tell yourself you have the skill or courage to go after what you want—these are all examples of good self-talk. Any words that make you feel inspired, worthy, and wonderful... those things? Awesome self-talk.

Now that you're aware of the difference, you must accept the responsibility that all of your self-talk—good or bad—is a *choice*. Your choice. You *choose* to use good self-talk or bad self-talk.

It sounds simple—"I'm gonna do GOOD self-talk from now on!"— but that doesn't mean it's easy for everyone. We'll get there though, don't worry. Saying nice things to yourself, about yourself, can be an adjustment for some, especially anybody with low self-esteem who's been using bad self-talk for a long time. The words can feel, literally, hard to say, because you're not used to speaking like this to yourself.

But I promise, once you start, it gets easier and easier.

The question then, is... now that you know you have this power, *how will you use it?* Contemplate this for a moment. Close your eyes and feel it. Take a moment and think back to the last time you looked in the mirror. What did you think or say to yourself? When you dressed and brushed your teeth this morning, did you feel love toward yourself and your body? If so, that's great—high five! Keep it up, because that creates a day full of excitement and opportunity. You're going to jump into Coffee Self-Talk with both feet, I know it!

However, maybe it wasn't that rosy. Was your self-talk negative? Did you criticize yourself? Did you pick on yourself? If so, you're creating negative energy that follows you throughout your day, like Pig-Pen's swirling cloud of dirt and bugs. Don't worry, it's ok. Well, it's not ok... it's *normal*... but what I mean is, don't worry, we'll fix that. Coffee Self-Talk to the rescue! Self-talk can be used to create a whole new you, a new personality, and that's exciting news!

The cool thing is that, as you think your new kick-ass thought patterns, over time, the old thoughts wither away because you're using them less. Connections in your brain literally shrivel up from disuse, just like muscles. As the old saying goes, "Use it or lose it."

In other words, the more good things you say and think, the more your brain changes to support those things, while getting rid of the old, unused connections. When this happens in the brain, neuroscientists call it "pruning," which is a wonderful metaphor... just imagine all the old, bad garbage being pruned away, like dead branches on a tree. *Snip. Snip. Snip.*

That's why the more you use self-talk in a positive way, the more you'll feel positive. You train yourself into feeling this way. For example, when you tell yourself that you are a great, likable, and cool person—every day—you're wiring that thought in your brain. And while you're doing that, you're not saying something negative because the brain only focuses on one thing in any moment. The more you say the good stuff automatically means the less you'll say the bad stuff.

When that happens, your life changes dramatically because you start to attract more feel-better things and positive people into your life.

How to Have Awesome Self-Talk

Fixing your self-talk can be as simple as thinking to yourself something like, "I'm really cool and kind." Or, "I am a good friend." Or, when someone says, "Hi, how are you doing?" You reply with a big response like, "I'm super!" or "I'm incredible!"

This might feel weird at first. Over-the-top, silly, dorky, and strange. But it's not! The more times you do it, I swear, the more fun it gets, especially when you watch people's reactions. I love it when someone asks me how I'm doing, and they're expecting the typical, "I'm fine," but then I blast them with an *"I'm incredible!"* Or even... *"I'm freakin' fantastic!"* It's funny when they do a double-take. After the brief shock wears off, they can't help but reply with a bit of awe, "Wow. Um, that's cool." (That's always a fun social experiment.)

After any strangeness wears off, these positive replies become your new comfortable norm. And then, if you don't respond with a big, positive affirmative, you actually won't feel quite right, like something is missing. But during the initial phase, when positive affirmations still sound strange coming out of your mouth, the thing you need to realize is that *you don't really have to believe the words at first.*

In time, you will! That's the magic of self-talk.

In fact, the way you feel today—good or bad—is the result of brain-programming words you've received in the past, from parents, teachers, friends, television, social media, etc. And, in particular, words you've thought or said to yourself.

Fire It Up to Wire It Up

When you do something (or feel something) over and over, it becomes baked into your head. The common expression is that your brain cells "fire and wire" together with the thoughts you have. This means they activate by firing, with a certain thought pattern you think, and every time they fire together, the neurons start to connect, or "wire together."

Fire it up to wire it up!

The more this happens—or the more intense the emotion that accompanies the firing and wiring—the stronger the connection. It's why some memories are so prominent, because of the level of emotion that happened at the time of the event. But it's also why some things always cause you to feel a certain way, because over time, you've thought and felt the same way about that thing—over, and over, and over—and it becomes your default. You've fired it enough times that it's become wired.

Using this amazing knowledge about how the brain builds itself, we can fire and wire thoughts for the most incredible life. Do this enough times, and the pattern becomes deeply ingrained, as though the wires were thicker and stronger. When you focus your attention on new thoughts for a few minutes a day, you'll build sparkly, tough new connections. They will become the new you.

Self-Talk Is Like Baking a Chocolate Cake

Think of the self-talk process like you're baking a chocolate cake.

If you want to make a chocolate cake... are you going to put liver into the batter? No! Are you going to throw in some grass clippings? No! Are you going to add pasta? No!

What are you going to put into it? You're going to put in *chocolate cake ingredients* because you want a chocolate cake. You know, flour, eggs, chocolate, sugar, butter... the results you desire come from the ingredients you use.

It's the same with your life experience. If you want a happy life, or success in school or sports, or great friends, then you must start with the right ingredients: the right self-talk. This good, positive self-talk brings you those good, positive results you deserve.

Remember, you're free *in every moment* to think life-uplifting and powerful thoughts (those chocolate cake ingredients)... or not. You can choose. Every choice is a chance to make change. To make the best cake!

Sooooo... How Is Your Self-Talk These Days?

I'll tell you the truth about myself. I was pretty shocked when I took the time to listen to my own self-talk, once I learned that it was the key to the kingdom of magical living. It was a huge moment for me, because, you see, I'd thought I had good enough self-talk.

But ohhh noooo, I wasn't even close. My self-talk actually kinda sucked.

When I first learned that *everything we say is an affirmation of some type*, that it's either a positive or a negative affirmation, and that it creates my life experience, I took a hard look at the words I was saying to myself every day. Each word, every thought.

Even though I thought a lot of positive things about myself, in general, I was jolted to discover I actually thought many negative things, too. I was a harsh critic of myself. It could be about anything... a zit, a bad hair day, frumpy-looking clothes, food I was eating, the money in my bank account, the people around me, etc.

Despite being a generally positive person (or so I thought), I sure managed to find an awful lot to complain about. Even if these were micro-complaints, they slowly chipped away at my self-esteem, my health, my happiness, and my life experience.

But I didn't know that!

And that's where it can be sneaky. You see, I had enough good self-talk going on in my life that my bad self-talk wasn't completely detrimental. But I didn't realize how much better things could be.

Let's say my self-talk on a typical day included 87 negative and 153 positive instances. The positives dominate, making me feel more positive than negative, so my self-talk wasn't negative enough to make me feel the need for change. But just one of those negative points affects my brain negatively, in the short term and long term. *Just one!* I didn't realize that *every* negative thought shuts you down, even if just a bit. These add up and lead to sucky consequences. Opportunities vanish, like the light when the power goes out. Or like a magician's trick, where the rabbit is here and then gone—*poof!*

This was eye-opening for me. This moment of self-reflection, this insight, was a briefly tender and sad moment, as I realized how I'd been treating myself badly for so many years. *But...* it was also super encouraging! Now there was so much room for improvement! *Woo-hoo!*

There were now tons of opportunities to uplift myself. This insight lit a shimmery fire in my belly, and I fully embraced how my life was going to change, once I cut out the negative crappy-talk and replaced it ALL with positive words. *And I mean ALL!*

Because, the truth is, we don't need *any* negative self-talk. Nada. Zilch. Each instance, no matter how small, has a price. It's death from a thousand cuts... it doesn't slay you in a single negative instance or thought, but you slowly die a little more in your heart with each harmful word.

But when you have positive self-talk as your default, it's like a super-protective, nutrient-vitamin infusing your body with diamond brilliance. It's not mystical either, even though some of the words in my self-talk might seem so. I'm just using magic-sounding words to paint a colorful picture for my brain to start making real.

Dance Your Own Dance Starting Today, No Matter What

I don't know if you realize this, but you have *tremendous power* when you're not dependent on the conditions in your outer world to make you feel good. You have tremendous power when your thoughts and emotions are not subject to what other people do. When you're not being whipped around by your ponytail because someone else has a hold of it. Because, no matter what is going on outside your head, you control the inside... your thoughts and feelings.

Your self-talk is important because what you think about yourself becomes your "truth." Your truth becomes your life, your destiny. In fact, how you feel about yourself is the driving force behind whether you have a good day, a ho-hum day, or a dark day. Think about it... how you feel right now is the result of how you thought about yourself this morning, yesterday, last week, and last month.

Imagine you're standing in front of a door. It's closed right now. On one side is your amazing life, filled with light, love, confidence, excitement, shooting stars, and your dreams coming true. On the other side is YOU. You stand there, hand on the knob. All it takes to open that door is for you to think "door-opening" thoughts. It's like a Jedi power. You say positive, uplifting things about yourself and your life. The door's handle turns golden and shimmers with warmth from the energy you transfer to it. You feel uplifted with these thoughts you're now telling yourself, and the handle turns. So easily, too. You open the door and walk through it, to everything you always wanted to be. It's all you... *you* were the key to the magical kingdom.

This truth was always there, just waiting for you to take the step.

Close your eyes. Feel it. The light... it has always been there. It will guide you.

— Man Kanata

Chapter 3

LIFELONG HAPPINESS

When I started waking up with a smile, I knew I was on to something with my Coffee Self-Talk. I had more purpose, focus, and fun. Instead of dragging my feet to the bathroom to brush my teeth, I skipped or danced, ready to see what the day had in store for me. And that's one of the best benefits about all this: loving your life more.

Would you like to have a smile on your lips more often? Now you can. When you improve your thoughts, you start making your dreams come true. On the surface, the affirmations might seem like they're just words, but their effect on you goes much deeper. This powerful, inner conversation of yours fixes, shapes, and reprograms your mind, and actually changes you into a dynamic, new person.

It's time to shine bright, like the beautiful star you are. Once you start, you'll know exactly what I'm talking about. Things will start to change, some small and some huge. You'll find yourself easier-going, less judgmental, and way happier. That's how it begins for all of us.

And then, you get on a roll, and so many crazy-cool things start happening, you can't help but pinch yourself. You get new ideas. Your creativity flourishes. You'll find yourself able to do things you never thought possible.

Like me, when I literally *talked myself* into becoming an author of romance novels. Seriously.

My Unexpected Journey to Becoming a Novelist

I never thought of myself as a creative person. I mean, the most creative I got was with cooking, when I'd make up new recipes. But I never learned how to draw or paint, and I certainly never wrote fiction. In fact, when my daughter was born, I begged my husband to be in charge of story time at night because I just didn't have any stories in me.

Or so I thought!

A few years ago, when I started doing Coffee Self-Talk, just for fun, I decided to throw in a few affirmations about being a good writer. Here are the exact words I added to my daily Coffee Self-Talk script.

I am a creative genius.

I have tons of stories to tell.

I am a prolific writer.

And that was it.

Now, I haven't shown you many examples of affirmations yet, or explained about writing your own scripts, but to give you an idea, my usual Coffee Self-Talk script had a variety of affirmations ranging from being fit and healthy, to making money, to living a great life, to feeling happy, and all kinds of cool stuff. And I change them frequently. So there was nothing unusual about adding three new lines. What was different was that I had never previously used any affirmations about creativity or writing stories. I just added them into my regular Coffee Self-Talk script one day, and then went about my business.

Fast forward five months. I'm sitting in my mom's backyard under the hot Arizona sun, when COVID was just starting to get bad, and suddenly, an idea for a story popped into my head.

WHAT?

I had an idea for a story!

I laugh about it now. I was so shocked by the story forming in my mind that I literally turned around in my chair and looked behind me to see where the idea had come from. Like, *who me?*

Over the next few weeks, I became a fire hose of story ideas, dozens of them, despite never having written a word of fiction in my life.

That was in 2020, and on the same day that first story idea popped into my head, I started researching how to write novels, devouring everything I could find on the subject. (If you're curious, email me, and I'll share how I got started.) And guess what? That year, I not only wrote my first novel... I wrote *nine* novels. Nine! In one year! It was friggin' nuts! I was *on fire*.

All because I told my brain, *I am a creative genius, I have tons of stories to tell, and I am a prolific writer.*

I kept telling my brain those lines every day. And my brain made it happen. Now I love writing more than anything I've ever done. It's so fun!

Here's another cool thing about self-talk. It not only makes great things happen in your life, but it also helps when not-so-great things happen. So listen up. If you have anxiety or fear in life, rest easy because you now have a tool in your toolkit to help. (See Chapter 20 for more on anxiety, and kicking it to the curb.)

When you start living your life with your new positive self-talk and your new great mindset, those anxieties and fears won't have as much power over you, *because you'll know how to move through them,* easing the load and feeling better, moment by moment. Sometimes I think of Violet's forcefield superpower (from *The Incredibles*), with her ability to create a purple ball of energy around herself. Self-Talk is awesome like this. Things that used to be a big storm raging through your life, causing destruction, are now just a breeze that almost tickles as it passes by. Or bounces right off your purple forcefield.

And, by the way, you'll likely experience far fewer problems in the first place. To understand why, you need to know about the *energy boomerang...*

The Trick to Lifelong Happiness: Your Energy Boomerang

Happiness in life is all about energy. And whatever energy we put out attracts the same kind of energy back to us.

You put out energy.

I put out energy.

We all put out energy.

Love has an energy. Success has an energy. This is key to loving your life. Why? Because the formula basically goes like this: Things in the universe with the same energy like to hook up with each other.

For example, when I wake up happy, I smile more because I feel an uplifted energy. And when I head outside into the world with a smile on my face, do you think people are more likely to approach me or be repelled by me, versus when I'm scowling or indifferent? When I smile, they're more likely to approach me! And why is this important? Because it brings opportunities to me. New friends. More happiness. You know what's not likely to come my way? Angry people putting out their own nasty energy. Because our energies don't like to tango. Which is fine by me!

So the obvious question... what determines the kind of energy you put out?

YOU DO!

Your thoughts are energy. Your feelings are energy. So, the thoughts and words that play in your head all day, and the feelings that match those thoughts, these put out a particular energy. Some people call it a vibration or a *vibe*. And this vibration will attract more of the same vibration. Like a boomerang, whatever you put out comes right back at you. An energy boomerang!

You already know this to be true. When you walk into a classroom or a party, and you see somebody with a good vibe, you feel it. You know it. And you notice that other people are drawn to that person, because they like the vibe he or she is putting out. That person is engaging and happy. It's attractive. It's compelling. And it makes you feel good to be around it. It draws you in.

On the other hand, if you know someone who's regularly angry, or complaining, or whiney, they're putting out a negative vibe, and you know that never feels good to be around... unless, of course, that matches your vibe. In which case, you might actually like being around them because you don't feel so alone, or because they're worse off than you, which actually makes you feel better about your situation. But even so, deep down, it's not how you really want to feel because it's not fun. It's not epic living!

So here's the important takeaway. Coffee Self-Talk helps you live an amazing, happy life because your words, thoughts, and feelings create a vibe that radiates off you, looking for similar vibes in your world to hook up with. When your vibe is high and awesome, you attract more high and awesome things and people to you. It's how I attracted the most amazing husband.

I love how reliable this is. I love knowing that when I put out good energy, and my focus is on good things, I'm attracting what I love and want. Things start to line up. They start to *click*. I see opportunities everywhere. Life becomes fun! There's less stress, more creativity, and more sparkles.

You can draw more goodness into your life by thinking and feeling good thoughts, because of your focus and energy. This includes health, success, love, happiness, and more.

When You Set Goals, Your Brain Rewards You!

I'll share a cool thing about your brain... it rewards you for setting goals.

What? How?

When you set a goal, it makes your brain expect something, which causes your brain to release an amazing chemical called dopamine. *And this chemical feeeels really good.*

So what I'm saying is, *you actually feel good when you set a goal* because of dopamine going *squirt squirt squirt* in your brain. And then, get this! When you take a step toward reaching that goal, more dopamine. *Squirt squirt.* More feeling good.

This amazing neurotransmitter, dopamine, fuels you with energy to take steps to get the thing you want. What does this good feeling feel like? It feels like energy, like motivation, like propelling, like magic. There's a reason the brain does this. It allows us to meet our needs. It helps us survive.

How about that? Now you have an incentive to set goals, knowing it'll feel good from the moment you set them, and then also with every step you take toward the goal. So when you set goals to make great friends, or get awesome grades, or improve in your sport, or send off college applications, your brain hooks you up with good feelings. It encourages you with dopamine to motivate you to keep taking steps in that direction! Brilliant!

The energy of the mind is the essence of life.

— ARISTOTLE

Chapter 4

LIKING YOURSELF… A LOT!

So now you know that your Coffee Self-Talk includes thinking and saying nice things to yourself. But what you might not have known is that you end up actually *being* kinder to yourself, liking yourself more and more each day, until eventually you're crazy in love with yourself in the most beautiful way.

For example, consider a girl who isn't happy about her looks. But despite this, she starts doing Coffee Self-Talk and affirming love for herself every day. This isn't how she usually thinks about herself, but she's willing to give the affirmations a try. Previously, she would complain and sigh whenever she saw herself in the mirror. Or avoid looking at herself altogether. But now, she has started thinking and saying better things to herself—she is determined to shine brighter, and shine that light back on herself with a new way of talking to herself.

She starts by simply saying "hi" to herself in the mirror every time she goes into the bathroom. This is powerful because she's validating her presence. Like, "Hi, you matter." Then, she gives herself a friendly smile. After a few days of doing this, she starts saying in her Coffee Self-Talk, *"I like myself."* Even though she might not yet believe the statement, she says it anyway, because she knows it's firing and wiring new beliefs into her brain. These will soon become her truth.

Then, she starts to notice a slight shift. She finds herself being gentler with herself, kinder, and criticizing herself less. After another week or so, she actually starts to think she's prettier than she's ever been. Her kindness toward herself, spoken consistently, has begun to bounce back, so she now actually begins to see herself in a radiant new light.

The really crazy part—the *magical* part—is that she actually *is* prettier now... literally more attractive to other people. You see, humans are finely attuned, mostly subconsciously, to the subtlest of changes in someone's physical presence: facial expressions, posture, poise, mannerisms, speech, confidence, and so on. When loving, radiant light starts to flow from you, *people notice!*

For some people, this transformation will be a bit slow-going at first. Saying the words might seem insincere—or even ridiculous—and that's 100% ok. Keep up the effort. It *will* work... you just have to give it time. You *will* change. More love will flow through you, and from you, because that's how the brain works. Remember the firing and wiring principle? Your job is just to keep on firing thoughts, and over time, your brain will wire those thoughts for you, making you feel them as truth, which then starts putting out that boomerang energy I mentioned in the last chapter.

As you start to feel love for yourself, it makes your dreams easier to attain because you really start to *believe in yourself.* It boosts your confidence, and you start enjoying your day more, because you believe that good things can happen. And this belief means good things actually *can and do* happen. You feel secure, and so you're willing to take more chances. You find yourself smiling more and taking on more challenges, which makes your day more exciting!

A Super-Duper Important Thing to Note

The key point is to like yourself as you are, now. Meanwhile, you'll tell your brain how to create the new you that you want to become. For example, you don't want to wait to like yourself after you lose weight, or have better skin, or have more friends, or get better grades. Rather, you love yourself *as you are now,* and then watch as the weight effortlessly sheds, or your skin takes on a beautiful glow, good people are drawn to you, and getting better grades becomes easier, as a result of your radiant, new self-identity.

Why does this work?

It's simple.

In addition to the firing and wiring happening in the brain, your *behaviors* automatically start to change. These actions follow the new directions you've given your brain, based on the words you say during your Coffee Self-Talk.

You see, when you love yourself *as you are now,* you make choices to support that love of yourself and your body. And those choices are effortless. They're not stressful. They don't require discipline. They're just how you naturally want to behave, once you've rewired your brain.

By loving yourself now, you might, for instance, start choosing to eat healthier foods, sometimes *without even realizing it.* Your subconscious does all the work. This is because a person who loves her body naturally won't want to abuse it.

In short, *when your self-talk changes, your behavior changes.*

Or think about this... maybe you opt for that bag of salt and vinegar chips, because, yes, you love yourself, and they're delicious, and so you're going to enjoy them by eating them. That's ok, too, and here's why: You'll love yourself the whole time you're eating it, with each bite, savoring, and there is *no guilt.* That is powerful, too!

The first example is obvious; you chose healthy food, and it helped make you healthier. The second example—the salt and vinegar chips—is less obvious. When you have so much joy and love for yourself, there are no thoughts of guilt, no negativity, no stress hormones, and your body assimilates the food lovingly and healthfully.

Of course, I'm not suggesting we scarf down chips every day because we love ourselves so much, but you see, that would never happen anyway because of the first example. When we love ourselves, it changes our behavior to make better choices, and when we choose better, we live better. Eating chips every day would be inconsistent with your self-loving identity, and you wouldn't have the urge to do something that's harmful to yourself.

Here's another example, but this one is about relationships: You don't wait to find someone to love you before loving *yourself first*. When you love yourself first, then you can relax and just chill out as someone wonderful comes into your life, as if by magic. Loving people are attracted to loving people. When you send out the right energy—the right *vibe*—other people will notice and find your energy irresistible. Literally... they can't resist it. They *must meet you*. Must get to know you. This applies to friends, romance, and future business relationships.

Here's a rule to live by:

> *Loving yourself is required for manifesting your dreams.*

Something amazing happens when we love ourselves. Everything brightens, shimmers, becomes lighter, yet stronger. An unseen weight is lifted off our shoulders when we give ourselves permission to do what is our birthright: Loving ourselves. We feel better instantly, no matter what is going on in life. A breakup? A pandemic? A problem at home? A hurtful comment from someone? That's ok, because loving yourself keeps you feeling whole. Loving yourself keeps you feeling worthy. When you feel worthy, you're absolutely unlimited. Unstoppable.

Initially, loving yourself might seem hard to do. But that's where Coffee Self-Talk comes into play and guides you. While doing your Coffee Self-Talk, you're pumping yourself up, changing the wiring in your brain, and in turn, starting to love yourself. It might not feel like that the first time you sit down to read your Coffee Self-Talk, but after a few times, it will start to take root. You planted seeds, you watered and nourished them through repetition, and the sprouts take root. Soon, you'll start noticing that your life just seems to get better and better, and your possibilities and opportunities grow and grow.

Is Self-Love Just Narcissism?

Narcissism is excessive admiration of oneself. Some people ask, isn't self-love the same thing? No, it's not. In fact, it's almost the exact opposite. You see, narcissism actually comes from a feeling of fear and inadequacy. In its extreme version, pathological narcissism is a personality disorder characterized by severe selfishness, a need for admiration, and the belief that the individual is more deserving than everyone else.

Self-love isn't that at all. With self-love, we know everyone is worthy of living the most amazing life.

But here's the thing... extreme narcissism is the result of a *deep sense of self-loathing*, in which the ego protects itself by artificially propping itself up, to absurd degrees, and to the detriment of everyone else.

Truly confident people don't brag; they feel no need to. Nor do they crave attention. Or feel the need to always be "right." Whenever you see somebody acting like this, what you're actually witnessing is a frightened ego seeking external validation.

In short, narcissism is based on fear.

Self-love is the opposite.

Many positive self-talk affirmations (and the Coffee Self-Talk scripts in this book) build upon the concept of self-love, which becomes the rock-solid foundation upon which lasting, positive change is possible.

Without self-love, it is very difficult for people to see themselves as *worthy...* of receiving what they want. And they'll often, unconsciously, self-sabotage their efforts, such as by procrastinating, or failing to follow through.

For this reason, the Coffee Self-Talk scripts in this book contain many *self-love* and *self-affirming* affirmations, such as:

I'm a beautiful and creative genius.

I am brave.

I love me.

I am magnificent. I am magical.

I am confident and shine like a star.

And so on.

Lines like these are designed very specifically to program your brain with self-love and self-belief. They are your *self*-talk... they are not what you go around telling the world. That is, unless your intention is to teach others how to do it, or to spread the idea of self-love, or set an example, such as to friends and loved ones. They are not boasts. They are never meant to be used to try to impress others.

Once you have programmed your brain to believe, *and feel,* thoughts such as these, they will become part of you and manifest in all kinds of ways, some of which will be apparent to the world, and many of which will not, because they will only show up in your own internal, blissful, happy, magical state-of mind. Which is the furthest thing possible from the internal state of a narcissist.

Here's a cool thing about other people though, like friends or family. When you start shining your light, you give them permission to shine theirs. If you have a sibling, don't be surprised if they start looking at you differently. They'll know you're up to something. Share it with them, with love. If they're not into it, no worries, you just keep on shining. But then don't be surprised if, later, they ask you about it again.

Why?

Because they've seen the happiness that you have, *and they want it, too!*

> *A person is what he or she thinks about all day long.*
>
> — RALPH WALDO EMERSON

Chapter 5

BULLETPROOF CONFIDENCE

My own self-talk has increased my confidence to such a healthy degree that I now easily talk with strangers, striking up conversations more comfortably than ever before. Even in Italy, where I don't yet speak the language very well—I approach people with no fear about screwing up or being misunderstood. This not only helps me learn more (Italian, in my case), but it also opens up many new opportunities. Sometimes I learn things or meet people that solve an immediate problem in my own life, or I tap into a whole new network of people from a single conversation with one stranger. Or I discover a way I can help them with something, or maybe I just make a new friend. It's always a win.

This confidence also enables loving myself through any stress and anxiety, instantly creating a safe place to be. When I used to write a blog post or publish a book, rather than feeling joy from my accomplishment, I was filled with anxiety. Because, once my written content was out there, I felt vulnerable. I wondered how it would be received. I kept checking social media with squinted eyes... did people like it? Did they hate it?

Not any more... to hell with that! Now, I courageously push my art into the world with joy and excitement. I've conditioned my mind to know that I'm a prolific writer with plenty to offer the world. And that it comes from an unlimited wellspring of creativity. I can keep creating non-stop, because there's no lack of creativity... the words just flow and flow and flow from my fingertips into the keyboard. I keep telling myself that—*and it works!*

I also have incredible resilience as well. I no longer worry about other people's reactions. Some people will like my work, and some people won't. The people who like it are my audience; those who don't aren't. For my part, I'm having so much damn fun writing and sharing, that I'm excited and eager to keep doing it.

You're here on Earth to do something special. You're here to live *your truth*, and create or do whatever it is that you are led, drawn, and excited to do. You were born to have the best friggin' life imaginable. Your self-talk will increase your confidence in this belief and create a saucy, magical, feel-good stew where self-reliance and resilience are just a regular part of who you are.

Once you've used your Coffee Self-Talk to reprogram yourself to be confident, you will no longer need to consciously think about it. It becomes your "new normal," your new way of being. This is when true mastery and power are at your fingertips. Your default mindset becomes one of flexibility and confidence. Like a palm tree in a trop-ical storm, it stays rooted, effortlessly bending in the wind—dancing —until the howling wind passes. These things allow you to handle any situation and resist fear. It's epic. It's game-changing.

You'll find that your positive self-talk is a healthy and nourishing habit because it helps keep your emotions in check. You're not easily upset by external events or your own random thoughts. Your self-esteem becomes too strong for that. External conditions and opinions of others, like kids in school, or a coach or teacher, will have less weight, as your internal value (your self-esteem) increases. When this happens, bullets bounce off you (well, the metaphorical kind), giving you the strength and resilience to get up again and keep on going.

Besides, you can't control others. And that's fine. They're in control of their own minds and their own experiences... just like you get to be in charge of your own mind and experiences. (I talk about peers and relationships a lot more in Chapter 18.)

This flexibility, this endurance you'll have... is one of the most important benefits of Coffee Self-Talk. You gain the courage and confidence to strive, reach higher, and take chances. Like having the confidence to ask that special someone out on a date, to ask for that raise you deserve at work, to negotiate with your parents, to post that video on YouTube, apply for that scholarship, or audition for that play. Or hey, even writing that novel! Failure becomes impossible because, no matter what the outcome, you learn and grow from the experience. Either way, you're no longer afraid of rejection, and you look forward to attempting new challenges and learning from them.

This whole new you gives you a powerful self-reliance. If there's something you don't know, no problem... you know how to get the answers, whether that means diving into Google or asking someone for help. This is true self-reliance. And it's the result of your self-talk, which I'll be showing you exactly how to do very soon!

The mind is everything. What you think, you become.

— THE BUDDHA

Chapter 6

SMASHING GOALS

News flash!

Coffee Self-Talk can help you attain your goals.

The reason I'm so intense about making my Coffee Self-Talk a daily ritual is because, when I decided I wanted to become wealthy, I aimed to make it happen *as soon as possible*. And nothing makes things happen faster than consistent, daily progress. I realized that all the things I'd done in my past—good or bad—were really just lessons and experiences, and I was free to live differently the moment I chose to do it. Nothing would hold me back. I was determined.

It doesn't matter where you are in your life, at this moment as you're reading this book. If you've made mistakes, or if you feel behind in school, or if you have regrets because of past choices, none of that matters now. Because it all changes today, with this book, and with your new self-talk. Every day is a new you.

Your next level is ready and waiting for you. You'll start it with saying your new intentions and goals. You will transform. And you will watch the magic happen from the new spells that *you* cast.

Self-talk is a vital component to smashing through your goals, because it keeps your attitude and self-esteem boosted. It keeps you chugging forward like a freight train. Every. Single. Day. Remember that the positive words and thoughts you say (and think) are commands that you give to your subconscious mind. They're instructions, like a blueprint, for your brain to follow, and as you fill your head with these thoughts, they soon become your habits. These good habits help you make steady progress. Over time, that steady progress is the thing that lets you attain your goals.

But there's more to smashing through your goals than your brain firing and wiring awesomeness into you.

There's a super important part of your brain that you need to know about...

The Reticular Activating System: "The RAS Wizard"

There are millions of bits of information coming at you at all times... from all of your senses, and even your own thoughts. There's so much information that your brain can't possibly begin to process all of it. Instead, it has to choose what to pay attention to, moment by moment, and filtering out the rest. At any point in time, you're only aware of a tiny fraction of what's going on around you.

Here's a neat little test to prove this concept. Prior to reading this sentence, were you aware of how the bottom of your left heel feels? You probably weren't. Now focus on your left heel. Is there pressure on it? Is it smooshed inside a shoe? Exposed to open air? Is it hot? Does it itch? And while you were thinking about these things, what was happening with your right earlobe?

You didn't know, because you were focused on your left heel.

See? You can't focus on multiple things at once.

Your attention is like a spotlight. It's bright, and you notice the details of whatever it's pointed at, but it can only be pointed in one direction at a time.

There is a small part of your brain that determines where this spotlight is pointed. It's called the Reticular Activating System, or "RAS." It's like the gatekeeper of what's allowed to enter your mind. Think of it like the wizard behind the curtain. It plays a profound role in helping you attain your goals because it filters what information you'll pay attention to, based on the intentions you set for what you want.

When you use your words and thoughts to set goals about things you intend to accomplish, your brain goes through a process, using the Reticular Activating System, where it connects things in the outside world (observations, news, opportunities, people you meet, etc.) with the things from your *inside* world (your goals, your thoughts, and your self-talk).

Whatever you think about and desire seeps down into your subconscious mind, and the more you think and feel about wanting something, the more connections your brain will create related to those intentions and goals.

Your brain then uses the Reticular Activating System to be on the lookout for anything that might help you attain those goals. It will notice new things, such as information, people, and opportunities that might have relevance. Stuff you never would have noticed before, just like you don't notice your earlobe until I mention it. These things that are important for helping you make your dreams come true, are made prominent by the RAS Wizard. It shines its spotlight on them and says to your brain, "Hey, look at this!"

This system automatically starts to refocus your attention when you speak your first words of self-talk. The RAS Wizard does not judge what you focus on, whether it's positive or negative... it doesn't care. It doesn't decide *what* you should focus on—getting a job, studying for exams, dating, exercise... whatever—because that's up to you. That ball is in your court. The RAS will simply go to work, helping you notice things in your outer world to help you accomplish the intentions you set with your inner focus through your words, thoughts, and feelings.

Can you see how powerful this is?

If you think about and focus on good things, then your brain will "see" positive things all around you. It will make you notice things that seem to prove you are correct: *Yep, good stuff all around... look at this example, and that, and that over there.* You'll see it everywhere.

On the other hand—remember, the RAS doesn't judge, it just looks for whatever you tell it to look for—if you think about and focus on crappy stuff, well, guess what? You'll start seeing *that* everywhere! Reality has not changed. There's no magic going on here. But *your* reality has changed, and it *feels* like magic. Just like the Jedi Qui-Gon Jinn said in *The Phantom Menace,*

Your focus determines your reality.

So, if you focus on bad stuff—about yourself, other people, school, the world, whatever—your RAS is going to bring you bad things. It thinks that's what you want. And so you start to see all this negative stuff. And it feels like everything is always going wrong. You'll feel like you have bad luck, that you're living a crappy life.

But all of this is actually great news!

Because, when your focus is on positive things and goals, your mind becomes filled with positive thoughts—like love, and kindness, and excitement, and happiness, and fun and gratitude—then the RAS Wizard follows those commands, powers up its mega-bright spotlight, and starts looking for great things to help you find positive outcomes and attain those goals!

It's funny though, the RAS even works for neutral things. For example, if you start working on a school project about butterflies, then you'll start to see more butterfly-related things. You might suddenly see a butterfly sticker on a locker that was always there, but you never noticed it. It could be a pair of leaves on the ground that resemble the shape of a butterfly. Or, of course, you might start to notice actual butterflies. That's just how the brain works. It'll filter the world around you based on your focus.

The Reticular Activating System *Advantage*

I'm telling you all about the RAS, and how powerful this little system in your brain is, to show you how you can take advantage of it. To explain why some people seem to have all the luck. When somebody is consistently "lucky," it's actually caused by three things. Because of their positive thoughts, words, emotions, and focus:

1. They're putting out a great energy that attracts great things to them.
2. They're more confident and happier because they have a healthy self-esteem and mindset.
3. Their Reticular Activating System is focusing their attention on all the things that will help them smash through their goals.

They're seeing paths forward, and solutions to problems, that are invisible to everyone else. Even subconsciously, in the form of hunches and intuitions. They develop what seems like a kind of intelligence for making *better decisions*. These decisions lead to better outcomes. And over time, better outcomes look like luck to the rest of the world.

The same goes for people with *consistently bad luck*.

Have you ever known anyone who just couldn't catch a break? Their car breaks down on the way to a job interview, AND they sprain an ankle, AND they get caught doing something they shouldn't have been doing... all in the same week? I think we all know someone like that. An occasional mishap now and then can be merely bad luck. But when bad "luck" is consistent over time, it's almost always the result of a string of bad decisions. That person's RAS is focused on the wrong things.

Fortunately, you have total power over your RAS. It will focus on whatever you want.

And the best way to do that is to start doing your Coffee Self-Talk, using words and thoughts designed to give you an incredible life. A life where you feel beautiful and amazing, and you set great goals that you love working toward.

Again, it will feel absolutely *magical*... but it's really just science.

But Wait, There's One More Thing...

In the next few chapters, I'm going to teach you exactly how to do self-talk.

But before we begin, I want to tell you that something special happens with all this awesome-sauce, goal-smashing stuff. When you start doing your Coffee Self-Talk, and you fill your mind with positive thoughts and feelings, *your motivation goes through the roof.*

It's a natural by-product of going through the process. In fact, you can amplify it even more by making it one of the lines in your Coffee Self-Talk: *"I have incredible motivation!"* And you will literally start to feel more motivation.

It might still seem crazy that *just words* can have such a strong effect, but that's what happens when you keep firing and wiring words and thoughts like that, repeatedly, into your brain. It has no choice.

But, really, the affirmation like the one above, plus all the other great ones you'll use, they make you feel so friggin' happy that you shoot for the stars. You'll *WANT* to set goals and go after them.

And girl? You will!

Now the fun part begins. I'm about to tell you how to actually do this stuff.

Read on!

> *The people who are crazy enough to think they can change the world are the ones who do.*
>
> — STEVE JOBS

PART II

HOW TO DO COFFEE
SELF-TALK

Chapter 7

LET THE COFFEE SELF-TALK BEGIN!

First! How to Do Coffee Self-Talk (the Super Short Version)

The short version only has two steps. They are so easy, you won't even believe it.

1. Make yourself a cup of coffee every day. (Or tea, or water... whatever is your thing.)
2. While you sit down to drink your coffee, spend a moment really savoring it, luxuriating in its deliciousness—while filling your brain with powerful, positive self-talk, which you can read from scripts that come later in this book, or that you write yourself. (You'll learn how to write your own self-talk in a bit.) For the best results, speak the words out loud.

That's it.

See? I told you it's easy. Drink coffee, say words. Done.

The first time you sit to read your Coffee Self-Talk script, it might only take one minute to complete. If this happens, and you still have coffee in your cup, simply read your script again. And again. And again. Keep going, until you're done with your coffee. Then, go about the rest of your day feeling uplifted, more confident, and with a positive focus. If you don't feel this effect on the first day, don't worry. Give it a few days or a week. Soon, you'll start to notice a difference.

The words you read in your Coffee Self-Talk scripts aren't just any words. They follow a few important rules. I'm going to spend the rest of this chapter teaching you the special way to write self-talk scripts for maximum success.

To give you an idea of what a Coffee Self-Talk script looks like, check out some of these examples that I use in my own, personal Coffee Self-Talk:

*I love life. I love my life. **I love me!***

I bless everything in my life right now. My coffee, my chair, my bed, my family, my friends, my whole life.

*I am an amazing person because **I am kind**, beautiful, and generous.*

Life is full of opportunities everywhere I turn. I'm going for it!

I sparkle. I shimmer. I shine. Wooooo-hooooo!

I love today because I'm in charge of my day. I make it what I want! I feel powerful.

***I'm having an awesome day!** I smile. I am excited about everything that will happen today.*

I'm a magnet for success, love, and everything I desire.

I let go of all fear right now. Woooooosh! I am confident!

I am taking responsibility for my success now, and for the rest of my life. I'm a woman on a mission.

I LOVE feeling so awesome! Yesssssssss!!!

These thoughts and feelings instruct my brain and body, like a blueprint, so I make better choices, make fewer mistakes, feel stronger emotionally, and love my life more than I ever thought possible.

When you read your own Coffee Self-Talk script, *you might feel some crazy results instantly!* Or you might feel some resistance. Or you might initially feel strange saying it. That's ok, totally normal, and not a problem. Just keep reading your Coffee Self-Talk every day. You'll soon become accustomed to the sound of talking to yourself, about yourself. In fact, it will become so normal, you'll soon *never* tolerate a bad thought or word about yourself. You'll be struck by just how *wrong* it feels, like sandpaper rubbing on satin.

The more you speak your self-talk out loud, the easier it is to do. It becomes fun and natural, and you'll look forward to it. You'll crave it like you crave your coffee. As it feeds your brain and mind with super-charged mental nutrients, you might even start to feel tingly, sparkly... it feels so good. If you have any moments of doubt or weird feelings, simply observe the thought, and say, "Thanks for stopping by, thought." And then keep going, because that's how you win!

As you continue saying your new self-talk, you'll start to change over the next 2–3 weeks. I'm talking *dramatic* change. As in, becoming a new person. Again, caterpillar-into-butterfly stuff. Your brain literally begins to rewire itself when you show up to do your self-talk every day. You cease to be the same person you were when you began.

How to Write Your Own Coffee Self-Talk

In this section, I cover the basics for writing your own Coffee Self-Talk from scratch. If you prefer not to write your own, or if you'd like to use pre-written examples to get started right away, many pre-written scripts are provided for you in Part IV of this book.

Here are the steps for writing your own scripts:

1. Get pen and paper, a journal, your computer, or your smart

phone with an app like Evernote or Notes. (I use the Notes app on my iPhone.)

2. Write 10 to 15 great things about yourself or *how you want to become*. There are a few special rules for this, so read on before you start writing. These 10–15 phrases will become your self-talk, and they can include your own kick-ass positive affirmations, lyrics from songs that light you up, inspiring quotes, etc. You'll use them every day, and you're free to make changes all the time.

3. Once your script is written, wake up, get your delicious cup of coffee, and sip it while reading your self-talk script. Read it over and over. *Rinse and repeat*, until you've finished drinking your coffee. Reading out loud is best, if possible, even if you're just whispering. Do this every morning with your coffee, making it your special Coffee Self-Talk ritual.

4. Enjoy the awesome day YOU just created.

The Coffee Self-Talk Rules

Rule #1: Write in First Person

Always write, speak, and think your self-talk in the first person (so, always use "I"). For example:

> *I am kind to others, and I happily share with others.*

First person is necessary for making it the easiest way to get straight into your own head, feeling it faster. You're telling your story, in your words, in your voice. "I" is the *self* in self-talk. The feelings from first person are more intense.

Rule #2: Write in the Present Tense

The second trick to creating powerful self-talk is to write it in the present tense. This creates a sense that it has already happened, or it's happening now. Not tomorrow, not next month, not next year. Do this *even if the thing you want hasn't happened yet.* Remember, you're doing this to reprogram your brain. You want your brain to start acting *as though* the thing you want has already become reality. You don't want to give your brain any excuses to put things off until "later."

For instance, in my own personal Coffee Self-Talk, I repeat, over and over to myself,

I am a happy, sexy, millionaire.

To be clear, as of this writing, I do not have a net worth of one million dollars. But it would be of little use to train my brain with words like "I will become a millionaire one day." This would do very little to put a million dollars into my bank account any time soon, if ever.

So I say it like it has already happened. *"I am a happy, sexy, millionaire!"* See how much more powerful that is? Compelling? Convincing? Write and speak your self-talk as though there's no time between saying it and when it happens. No space between you right now, and your accomplishments and feeling good.

The things you write about in your Coffee Self-Talk will range from accomplishments you see yourself making, to ways to make it happen, to how it all makes you feel. It's your epic, new truth, and you're attracting your desires by positively affirming it all. Got it? Speak as if it's already accomplished.

Is This Just Lying to Myself?

No, you're not lying to yourself, you're describing a future reality in terms your brain can act on. Lying is about deception. Self-talk has nothing to do with deception, it's about *intention*. It's no more of a lie than when an architect creates a beautiful drawing of a shimmering, glass and steel high-rise building she's designing. The drawing of the end goal is required for all of the builders to know *what* to build. And *how* to build it. Same goes for your brain. Self-talk affirmations expressed as an already-realized end goal are a powerful way to make your mind focus on taking the right steps to make these affirmations become true. I think of my self-talk as *my true future me,* and I attract that future faster when it's expressed as though it's already happened.

If one day you're having a difficult time with something, pick a line from your Coffee Self-Talk, and repeat it over and over, for a minute or so. One of my favorites is:

I am super happy.

I say it over, and over, and over—maybe sixty times (though I don't actually count)—and it starts to sink in, right then, during the stressful moment, and it *immediately* soothes me. It can actually help you become happier right then and there. So in that case, you made it your truth right then. Was that lying to yourself? No, it was you issuing commands to yourself, like a director on a movie set.

In other instances, when you're working on making a future thing happen for you, like maybe getting into the university of your dreams, well, the more you affirm it, the more likely *it is* to happen. Now, to be clear, saying it over and over doesn't guarantee the outcome, but it is virtually guaranteed to help you move in the right direction. Or at the very least, it helps prevent you from moving in the *wrong* direction.

But wait, there's more good news! Expressing your *future in the present tense* does a couple of other awesome things...

1. It makes the whole time between the time you affirm it and the time the results come, much more enjoyable. It's way more fun thinking about your success than stressing about it, which would only make it less likely to happen.

2. If you don't get the exact result you wanted, trust me, it often means something *better* is in store for you.

This idea takes some getting used to. It's not what we're usually raised to believe... that somehow *not* reaching a goal can be a better outcome than reaching it? Huh? But, you see, life is weird and curvy and exciting like that... you just *never know* where things will lead.

If you wanted to get into a certain university, because you thought it'd make you happy, because of what you thought it would do for you by going there, sometimes you find yourself on an alternate path that you never could have envisioned.

In which case, go with it, be excited, because it means something even better is on the horizon when you keep your energy high, and you vibe with happiness.

Get Your Magic Wand Ready & Brainstorm

"Brainstorming" is when someone (or a group of people) sit down and think up a whole bunch of ideas, or different answers to a question, or possible solutions to a problem. The idea is to crank out as many ideas as possible, without regard for how good the ideas are initially. By removing the judgment and not worrying about *quality*, it frees you to be creative and think "outside the box," with an emphasis on *quantity*. That is, generating *lots* of ideas. Only after you've come up with a lot of ideas do you then start narrowing them down based on how good or useful they are.

A great way to brainstorm about writing your own Coffee Self-Talk script is to start by thinking about your life now versus the dream life you want. If you could wave a magic wand and make any changes to yourself or your life, what would you do? And remember, when you're brainstorming, there's no judgement based on quality or how realistic something is... that step comes later. For now, there are no limits. Have fun with it!

Do you want to get really good at something? Like a sport, or playing guitar? Do you want better grades? Do you wish you had more confidence? Do you want to heal from an injury? Would you like to find love? Do you want to lose weight, or find the motivation to work out? Do you want to get into a particular university? Do you wish you were more popular? Do you wish you were funnier? More creative? Happier?

Your Coffee Self-Talk is about focusing on who you want to become. The new identity you want. The new attitude you want. The new energy you want to radiate. It can be anything you want.

Picture your new self. How do you look? How do you feel? Do you smile more? Do you stand differently? Walk differently? What do you wear? Think about what you want, who you want to become, how you want to live, and how you want to feel.

Below, you'll find a list of questions. Use them to discover more about who you are, what you like, and to create more focus on the things you want.

You'll see that I ask "why" after most of the questions. The "why" is almost more important than the "what." When you ask why, you really get down to the root of what drives and motivates you, and it helps you identify what you really want in life. And sometimes, when you get down to the root of it, you realize it's a nasty weed, and you want to yank it out! Or you realize you have some work to do on yourself, perhaps some improvements to make with your own self-love, and it only becomes clear once you discover the compelling "why" behind your "what."

For example, if someone wants to be really popular, the first thing I would ask her is, "why?" And if she's really honest with herself, the answer might be because she's lonely, or because she doesn't feel good enough as she is. Those are not healthy reasons to seek popularity. But her answer is helpful in that it reveals that she has some inner, self-love work to do. Once she has self-love and self-worth, she won't feel the need or desire for popularity. And, ironically, she'll probably end up with more friends. But now, it will have come from a good, healthy place.

So... are you ready to brainstorm?

Remember, no judgment, *and have fun.*

Get your journal or some paper and spend time with the following questions. Take as long as you want. (Over multiple days even, if you get really inspired. This can be a fascinating exercise.) Write anything and everything that pops into your mind. You can always change your answers later.

1. What are all the things that uplift me and give me energy? In other words, what things make me feel excited, and in awe, or epic, like I'm in a movie? Why do these things do that for me?
2. How can I have more of these things in my life?
3. What three things do I have the most fun with, or give me the most joy? Why do I have fun with these things?
4. What are my favorite ways to pass the time? Why?
5. What are some things I could do all day long without getting tired of them, because I love doing them so much?
6. What do I want more of in my life? Why?
7. What do I want less of? Why?
8. What do I want that I don't have now? Why?
9. Who has made a positive difference in my life? What qualities does that person have that I like?
10. Who do I want to be five years from now? (Describe this in as much detail as possible.) Why?
11. Where is my favorite place to vacation? Why is it my favorite?
12. If I could travel anywhere for one week, where would I go? Why?
13. If I could travel anywhere for one to six months, where would I go? Why?
14. What qualities in other people do I most admire? Why? What can I do to acquire these qualities myself?
15. If I could be super skilled at any activity or sport, what would it be? Why?

16. What are three new things I'd like to learn how to do? Why? (Answer *why* for all three.)

17. What are three things I already do that I'd like to learn how to do better? Why? (Answer *why* for all three.)

18. What are all the things I'm good at? (Make your list as long as you can. The items can be anything, like eating your weight in watermelon... kidding, sorta, I can almost do that... or cleaning your room, being organized, tennis, cooking, math, braiding hair, your favorite video game... for anything you are good at, from small to big things. Be bold with your list. Write it all!)

19. If I could have any career that I wanted, or any job, what would it be? (Provide multiple answers, if you like.) Why?

20. If I were an old person looking back at my life, what would I hope to have accomplished? (Feel free to provide multiple answers.) Why this thing (or these things) in particular?

Ok! Great job going through those questions. Now, you can use all those gems you uncovered to help write your own scripts. The idea is to think in terms of your dreams, and write down statements using words like:

"I love ____"

"I am ____"

"I feel ____"

Etc.

With your Coffee Self-Talk, you're basically going to tell your brain what you love, what you are, and what you feel... based on the way you WANT to be and feel. For example, if you want happiness in your life, you'll say in your script, "I feel happy!" (Remember, you're stating your intentions in the present tense, as if they've already happened.)

Here are some examples from my own Coffee Self-Talk:

1. I wanted to make a lot of money. So I told my brain, "I am a millionaire."
2. When I have a headache, I tell myself, "My head feels great."
3. Even though I'm busy working toward goals that have not yet come true, I tell myself, "I am living the life of my dreams."

See how easy that is? Just take the thing you want, and write down a sentence saying you've already got it, or are doing it.

Got it? Ok, good.

Next, I'm going to teach you a few pro-tips to make your self-talk *super* effective.

Chapter 8

PRO-TIPS

Now for some pro-tips to make your self-talk even more effective.

Pro-Tip #1: For More Success, Use the Word "Because"

Using the word "because" is a smart way to enhance your self-talk, and this is backed by scientific studies demonstrating its power. When you use (or hear) the word "because," you're more likely to comply with what's being said or asked of you. The words that come after "because" provide the reason to do it. It justifies motivation for the action because it indicates a strong cause-and-effect relationship.

Your brain pays attention when you use the word "because," and you give more importance to the self-talk. When you associate results and meaning with your self-talk, you're more convinced it'll help you achieve your goals. So, set yourself up for success, and use the word "because" throughout your script, *because it'll really help*. (Hehe, see what I did there?) You won't do this with every affirmation you create, but sprinkle in a few here and there.

Examples:

I exercise regularly because it makes me feel great.

I'm a great student because I stay focused in class.

I'm a great student because I have a phenomenal memory.

I am a good person because I am kind to others.

Remember, even if some of these are not true yet, that's ok, you'd say them anyway, as if they were true. And when you repeat them, over time, you start to believe it, and then it starts to happen!

Pro-Tip #2: Spark Joy with Glittery Details

The little details you add to your scripts are important. Any descriptive words, specific examples, or colorful metaphors will create a more emotional and vivid picture in your head, making the desired outcome crystal clear to your subconscious mind.

For example, instead of saying, "I am attending the university of my dreams," someone interested in astronomy might say,

> *I am working towards my B.S. in astronomy*
> *at the University of Arizona.*
> *I love feeling the warm sun on my face*
> *as I walk to class each day,*
> *where I learn about the secrets of the universe.*

See the difference? Painting a vivid picture makes it more real in your mind! And the realness of this picture—here's the magic part—actually makes you more likely to get accepted into that university, even years in advance, by rewiring your brain to make you more focused in say, a math class, for which your grade ends up on your transcript.

You might add an empowering lyric from a favorite song that makes you feel awesome. Or you could write a line about doing something physical every day, and add specific details. So, instead of saying, "I do something physical every day," you could say,

I do something physical every day,
such as walking, swimming, or doing ten pushups.

If you want to improve your study habits, you'd include lines of self-talk that create that image in your head. Maybe lines about your laser-sharp focus, your brain's amazing memory, how much you love to read, and how good you are at retaining information. For example,

Learning is my superpower.
I learn anything and everything I want with ease.

You might also picture yourself in your favorite study environment. What would that look like? How would it feel? How would you sit? And so on... add details to your Coffee Self-Talk, and get creative and play with the words you're using until they spark joy with you.

Don't worry about getting it perfect the first time. Your scripts will change over time as your Coffee Self-Talk evolves. You can always mix it up and try new things, experimenting to see what you like the most. Have fun with it!

When I write my self-talk, the first thing I write down is literally whatever comes to mind, no matter how goofy. And believe me, some of it is pretty goofy! And as I start to write more, it gets easier and easier, and I just let it all out. After a while, once I've written a dozen or so affirmations, only then do I start to edit, deleting some and tweaking others until they spark joy with me.

Pro-Tip #3: Choose Your Words

Here's a tip to help you increase the feelings and emotions behind the words: Choose *effective words*. Power words. Certain words are cues, or triggers. When chosen carefully, they transform "Meh... whatever" into *"Wow, that's it!"* The emotion you feel will make everything happen much faster, because doing your Coffee Self-Talk *feeeeels* good when you use super good words!

Feel, to make it real.

Here are some words that trigger higher emotions. Pick the ones that speak to you. Then, infuse them into your Coffee Self-Talk.

- Amazing
- Awesome
- Beaming
- Blessed
- Blissful
- Bountiful
- Bright
- Calm
- Capable
- Centered
- Clear
- Confident
- Colossal
- Cool
- Creative
- Definitely
- Delighted
- Eager
- Easy
- Ecstatic
- Empower
- First
- Focus
- Freedom
- Funny
- Genuine
- Glowing
- Guaranteed
- Happy
- Helpful

- Honored
- Incredible
- Inspired
- Instantly
- Joyous
- Laughing
- Light
- Lit
- Lively
- Luminous
- Natural
- Open-minded
- Playful
- Radiant
- Reflective
- Relaxed
- Sensational
- Smiling
- Spirited
- Spontaneous
- Sunny
- Super
- Tremendous
- Uplifted
- Vibrant
- Vigorous
- Wondrous

Simple Starter Script

Now that you've learned how to write some basic self-talk, let's put it all together. Below are two examples of a general, non-specific Coffee Self-Talk script. I say "general" because these two scripts are about overall happiness and living a good life, rather than focusing on specific things you want to work on. In Part IV, I share a bunch of specific scripts that help with different aspects of life, such as school, relationships, beauty, health, etc.

The first example script is fairly basic. If it looks familiar, it's because I gave you a preview of it in Chapter 1. I start with gentle and effective words. Sometimes, when people first start doing Coffee Self-Talk, it can seem weird, so using short phrases and simple thoughts makes an easy first step. Later, we'll elevate the basic script, giving it more intense and impactful words. But this basic version will give you some ideas to get started, in case you're totally new to the idea of self-love and boosting your self-esteem.

Go ahead and make your cup of coffee. Once you have it, sit down and read the following script. Pause for a moment after each line to let it sink in.

I am a good person.

I like today. I like my life.

I will have a good day today because I'm ready.

I make excellent grades, and only good lies before me.

I like feeling good.

I approve of myself because I have a big heart.

I love the power I have in my life to feel good with simple words.

I achieve because I persevere.

I choose to feel good about myself because I'm worthy.

I am pretty.

I always have a choice.

I'm healthy and strong.

I have a good attitude.

I love me just the way I am, right now.

When you're first starting out, the goal is to have your script be about 10 to 20 lines long. You can add more later. Remember, your affirmations are about things you want to be, and have, and do (or experience). You can write affirmations for your goals and dreams, but also for ways you want *to feel*. For example, one of your scripts might include the line, "I'm a successful, straight-A student," followed by the line, "I feel wonderful from the moment I awake, and I'm excited to start my day."

Are You Feeling Silly About This?

I'll be honest, the first time I read my Coffee Self-Talk script out loud, I felt like such a nerd... but only for about a minute. Then, I thought about all of the ridiculously successful people out there who are using this technique. I mean, if it's good enough for professional athletes, it's good enough for me. Self-talk is not new, and there are legions of people using it to kick major ass, accomplish amazing things, heal from diseases, achieve super fitness, and live incredible lives.

I wanted a piece of that, and realizing this is one of the ways you can transform and take life to new heights, I was all-in. I threw off my imaginary, taped nerd glasses and donned my superhero cape. *Game on!*

The interesting thing was seeing how my Coffee Self-Talk scripts evolved over time. In the beginning, my scripts were much like the script you just read above. Now though, I pump myself up so high, I damn near feel like I'm levitating when I read it! I *really* get into it.

Amping It Up! A More Advanced Script to Level-Up Your Coffee Self-Talk

The basic script above is a great place to start. Take it and use every word, or make any changes to it that resonate with you. In my own personal Coffee Self-Talk, I tend to use the words "awesome" and "amazing" a lot. I also tend to throw in some sparkly cuss words for emphasis, but they all come from a place of fun and joy, never anger or frustration. The point is for *you* to choose words and expressions *you* love. You can also make your script longer or shorter... whatever length you want.

Once you get started, it's fun, and you'll be so excited about the possibilities that you'll start thinking of new ways to speak powerfully, lovingly, and positively about yourself. It's your time to shine!

Here's a more amped-up version, dense with power words:

I am an amazing person because I am kind, beautiful, and generous.

I love today because I'm in charge of my day. I make it what I want! I am powerful.

I'm having an awesome day today! I smile brightly, and I'm excited about everything happening.

I'm taking responsibility for my success, now, and for the rest of my life.

I LOVE feeling so freakin' awesome! Yessssssssss!!!

Yesterday is the past, and I'm not attached to it. I learn from it and move on.

I'm ready to love me today—here and now. This creates a great moment for me and sets up my future for more success.

I love the power I have in my life to feel so super, simply with the words I speak. I am amazing.

I can achieve because I'm capable, creative, and worthy. I choose me, and I honor who I am.

My life gets more amazing every day. Life supports me in every way.

I approve of myself. I am in awe of my sparkling life, my learning, and my growth.

I have a ton of time for everything I want to do today.

There is love and light all around me. I am compassionate, kind, and loving toward myself and others.

I have a happy heart and a creative mind.

I'm super smart, and I love to learn.

There is no one else in the world like me.

I am full of optimism and passionate about my destiny.

As you write and edit your own Coffee Self-Talk scripts, new ideas and descriptions will start to grow in your mind. The more you think about the amazing life you're living, the more ideas come to you. You'll find yourself during random moments of the day having an idea, or a flash of insight, and wanting to jot it down in your notes to add to your script later. Be sure and do this whenever the inspiration strikes!

So, Are You Ready to Play Ball?

It's time to acknowledge the strength and power within you. Time to amp up the energy with uplifted feelings to turbo charge your Coffee Self-Talk and manifest your dreams faster. And the longer you're experiencing these elevated emotions and feelings, throughout your whole day, the more you draw your desires to you.

But! This is still just scratching the surface. Keep reading to learn how to create your own super *badass* Coffee Self-Talk program to make your dreams come true even *faster*.

Quick Recap: How to Write Your Own Coffee Self-Talk

- Write in the first person.
- Write in the present tense.
- Use the word "because" in some of your affirmations.
- Use details to create vivid pictures in your mind.
- Use uplifting, emotional words for a bigger impact.

Chapter 9

FASTER RESULTS WITH FEELINGS

Great! It's time. Once you've written your script, you're ready to do your Coffee Self-Talk.

But guess what?

There's a very, very special way *to do* your Coffee Self-Talk. It includes two ingredients:

1. Your thoughts, and
2. Your feelings

I've briefly mentioned the importance of positive thoughts and positive feelings, and why they help you attract your best life by altering the energy you put out.

Well, this is the part where you actually learn *how* to do that. And in the process, ensuring you get the fastest results possible.

Let's Begin...

One of the most important ways to make your self-talk extra successful is to elevate the emotions you feel inside your heart, to accompany the words you think with your brain. (Technically, your emotions happen in part of your brain, but they *feel* like they're in the heart, so we'll stick with this as a metaphor.)

This emphasis on emotions, and how your emotions connect with your thoughts is super important.

The words you say are as important as how you feel, and how you feel is as important as the words you say. If words are peanut butter, then feelings are jelly. If words are peas, then feelings are carrots. If words are Batman, then feelings are Robin. It takes two to tango. It's like a marriage. We want them both!

Positive Words (your thoughts) +
Uplifted Emotions (your feelings)
= Epic Experience

Merely thinking about the dreamy awesome life you want isn't the fastest way to make it all happen. It turns out that just coming up with a list of wants and desires puts you in the slowpoke lane to making your dreams come true. It's not a dead end, but it's not a rocket sled ride either.

The magic happens when you combine your dreams and goals with *great, happy feelings*—where you feel unlimited, excited, and full of love. It's this union between the *thinking* and *feeling* parts of your brain that creates the connection in your thoughts and actions, removes all the barriers (like self-doubt), and puts you in a Formula One car, racing toward your future legendary life.

When your heart is filled with these emotions, there is no room for fear. Just imagine how your life would be if you felt *no fear* because your heart was filled with *confidence and courage* instead!

The stronger the feelings, the more powerful your energy is in attracting what you want. So when you really dive into these feel-good feelings, while imagining your great life that's coming to you, you'll draw it all to you much faster. You want to get so deeply into it that it tingles, excites you, and fills you with awe, and makes you want to run, dance, and sing. *That's* using positive energy and feelings to make great things happen in your life. (In a bit, I'm going to share some awesome tricks to help you tap into these turbo-charged feelings, so read on.)

Self-talk delivered with low or neutral emotion warrants a grade of B. It's ok... words alone are surely better than not doing anything at all, but it's nowhere near the A+ level that comes from doing positive self-talk with corresponding uplifted feelings. Your results will happen much faster when you get your emotions aligned with the words you're saying.

Note: For some people, in the beginning, only the words will seem possible. The emotions will feel too foreign or unrealistic. If that's the case, no problem, just start with the words. Repeat your awesome self-talk over and over, even if you're not feeling it yet. In time, you will. I promise.

Again—because it bears repeating over and over—*it doesn't matter if the affirmation isn't true yet.* The brain doesn't know the difference. It just goes on rewiring itself, and it builds those wires thicker and stronger when there's emotion attached. Emotions are the brain's way of knowing, *"This is important. I should pay attention to this!"* It works the same way with encoding memories. The stronger the emotion, the stronger the memory.

Let's try an example. First, read the following sentence like a robot, with zero emotion:

"I am having the most awesome day today."

Now, close your eyes, and imagine what it would *actually feel like* to have the most awesome day of your life. Really feel it, down to your toes. If necessary, take a few moments to get into this frame of mind.

And then, while you're still imagining that level of awesomeness, say, with 100% full emotion:

"I am having the most awesome day today!"

Can you feel the difference?

Of course you can! That's your emotions doing their job! And think about it—you told your emotions what to do, and they obeyed your command! *You're in charge.* You always are. You only need to use the power you already have over that part of your mind.

Now, whip up some similarly empowered emotions and say, out loud, with passion in your voice:

"I live an amazing life with opportunities all around me. Everything I do is a success. I have one success after another."

That would *feel* pretty awesome, right?

Let's explore this some more. What does awe feel like to you? What does feeling *expansive* feel like? Tap into that feeling! If you're still not sure, what would it take to feel awe? Maybe it's witnessing the birth of a baby, or seeing an athlete do amazing things with their amazing skills—making a hole in one? Sinking a basket from half court? Or maybe it's seeing something in nature, like bioluminescent waves, or the aurora borealis! Do these things fill you with awe? If so, you know the feeling. See the image in your mind as you process each self-talk statement.

Your goal is to feel an elevated emotion *while* you're saying your Coffee Self-Talk. There are many uplifted emotions from which to choose:

- Love
- Awe
- Inspiration
- Joy
- Bliss

- Generosity
- Abundance
- Courage
- Confidence
- Gratitude
- Excitement
- Happiness

... the list goes on and on.

When you experience any of these feelings, you feel elevated. You can tap into any one of them while reading your Coffee Self-Talk. It's not necessary to go through all of them. Any one of those elevated emotions works to uplift your feelings, wire your brain with Hulk-strength wires, and make you feel great.

Level Up Your Language!

After everything I've already said about what words and feelings to use for the most success, it probably seems crazy that I'd have even more to say about language. But I do!

And this time, it's about being mindful *not to use negative language.*

You might think, well, of course I won't use negative language because I don't want to attract negative things. But here's the sneaky thing about language. Sometimes we use words or expressions that are common in our culture, or we use words with the intention that they're uplifting, but they might actually be sneaking in some stealth negativity.

Here's a story to illustrate the point. Ten years ago, I walked into an AT&T store to buy a new phone. The sales guy was telling me about an app he thought I should download. After ringing me up at the cash register, he said, "Remember to download the app I told you about."

I replied, "Don't worry. I won't forget."

He looked at me sternly from across the counter in his crisp khaki shirt, and said in a fatherly tone, "You know... you should change your language. Your brain is always listening."

I gave him my best stink-eye. "What?" *What is AT&T dude talking about?*

Undeterred by my stink-eye, he said, "When you use the word 'forget,' even though you put the word 'won't' or 'don't' in front of it, all your brain really hears is the keyword: *forget*. And you're more likely to do just that. Instead, you should say, 'I will remember.'"

"Oh. Um, ok." I took my phone and left the store, thinking the dude should stick to selling phones. But you know what? He had a point. And it has stuck with me all these years.

Today, I can't help but chuckle at this memory. A seed was planted in my head, and I still *remember* it. What he said makes perfect sense, that small word choices might make a difference. And "I won't forget" is just one example. If you pay attention to what you say, you'll find more. For instance, be mindful of using expressions like *"I can't wait"* to do something. This might seem silly at first, because that expression is so common and is always used to convey excitement, but there's an even better way to say it: *"I'm so excited to..."*

So level up! You might as well, because it has an impact.

Instead, say something like, *"I'm excited to do _____"* (fill in the blank).

It may seem like splitting hairs, until you try it. Say each of these examples out loud, and note the difference:

> *"I can't wait to go to college."*

As opposed to...

"I'm so excited to go to college."

See what I mean? There's an implied intention that's so much stronger with the word "excited."

Here's another example. Instead of saying,

"When I swing, I don't miss."

Try...

"When I swing, I knock it out of the park."

Again, see the difference? The second version gives your mind an actual image, an image of hitting the ball out of the park and succeeding. Whereas the first line, at best, has no real image to see. And at worst, it risks that you'll key on the word "miss," thus causing the image *of missing* to pop into your head.

It's a subtle but powerful way to control the images that pop into your brain.

Instead of saying *"I hope"* for something to happen," use the words, *"I intend"* or *"I expect."* When you hope for something, it can seem like a lost cause, or passive, with no intention behind it. But an intention makes your brain perk up and take note. And when you *expect*, well, your brain expects it to happen.

Drop the Following Word from Your Vocabulary Forever

While we're on the topic of language, let's all drop the word *"hate"* from our vocabulary. I don't even know the last time I used the word.

The word *hate* is so dark and angry, and it's filled with super-crappy energy. It's not a word that will ever help you make your beautiful dreams come true. I even told my daughter, when she was seven years old, I'd rather hear her cuss than to ever use the word *hate*.

Now, there can be things in the world that you strongly dislike—and I'm not suggesting you ignore this fact—but the word *hate* is so powerfully negative that it shuts you off from your own mental resources that allow you to intelligently address problems or difficult people.

When you're stressed out about someone or something, the different regions in your brain stop talking to each other. This is bad. In order to access your full creativity to solve problems, you need the regions of your brain to be open and creative. So, very simply, when someone uses the word *hate* (or if someone thinks about things with hate-filled emotion), they close off the regions of their brain that might have helped solve the problem.

If there's a bad situation, whether it's personal, like someone hurting you, or a global problem, like hunger, poverty, pandemic, or anything that one might understandably "hate," it's important to realize that the emotion of hatred is a *result* of pain, not the *solution* to it.

What is the solution?

Well, that depends on the problem. But the first step is to turn off the negative emotion so that your brain can get to work on constructive solutions. If you're tempted to think that the hate might motivate you, then flip it around, and consider how much more motivated you'd feel by *freeing yourself* or others from pain or suffering. Times when you experience elevated emotions like optimism, exuberance, freedom, and joy are when our brains are the most creative and resourceful.

So remember, when hate is the focus, the brain freaks out and shuts down.

If hate is the focus, the vibe you put out is dark and whacked-out, attracting more dark and crappy things!

This does not mean we allow people to be mean to us or to bully us. That is not acceptable. But how we *react* is under our control, and giving energy to your hate will *always* dull your shine. You can have things you dislike in the world, but keep your mind open, with positivity energy, about how to change those things, or make them (or people) better. Or coming to peace with the things you cannot change. This lighter and brighter approach helps you solve problems in a good way.

Important! If your safety is ever at risk because of someone (adult or peer), the first thing to do is to get help from a trusted adult.

But if someone is just not being nice to you (and your safety is not at risk), it helps if you realize that it's often because they don't like themselves, and they're acting out, or they're immature. No one with good self-esteem and self-worth behaves badly toward others. In this case, you still want to keep your energy positive, which means not spending time around this person or this situation, if possible.

Beyond that, the best response to mean or negative people is turning inward and cranking up your own self-love.

When you have an abundance of self-love, it starts to overflow, making it easier to deal with others, and forgive them, too. Even people who don't seem like they deserve it. You see, they usually need it that much more, as something in their past caused them to be the way they are.

If you're feeling generous, you can send out some of that love to that other person, maybe in ways they see (like saying something nice), or ways they don't (like giving them kind thoughts). I know, it's not easy to send someone love when that someone is uncool. But really, this isn't about them, it's about you. When you send out love, it has this weird effect where it makes *you* happier.

Letting go of hate is one of the best ways to make yourself happy. Hate is like a burden that people carry. When they toss it aside, everything becomes lighter and easier.

Focus on What You Want, Not on What You Don't Want

Here's one last example of leveling up your language, and this is a BIG one.

When you're thinking about things you want in life, don't think about them based on what you *don't want*. For example, if you have an old, beater car you don't like, and you want a new one, don't think, "I want a different car because mine sucks." Those are negative feelings, and they will attract less than ideal results.

Instead, focus on the thing you *do want*, like seeing yourself in a different car, one that you love. See how this changes your emotion from a feeling of discontent, to one of happiness? It's that uplifted feeling you're aiming for. It's what makes you more resourceful at getting the thing you want.

Here's another example: If you're worried that your friends might be talking about you behind your back, and you think, "I hope they don't talk behind my back," then it's actually more likely that *that* is exactly what's going to happen, because that thought creates defensive, negative emotions in you. You will start believing you see them doing it, even where it may not exist (the Reticular Activating System at work). You fill your head with imaginary worries and fears, which your friends will pick up on, and it might make them want to withdraw from you. You project an insecurity, and other people notice it. In this way, the thing you feared can actually become true *because* you feared it.

Instead, think of happy thoughts about your friends. Confidently imagine the fun you have with them. See you all having a great time together and doing lots of fun things. And if, by chance, they actually are talking about you? Well, who cares? Don't give them any negative fuel. In no time, maybe they'll be wondering why you're so happy all the time. The point is, one of the key requirements of being a likable person, is that you don't worry too much if you're likable. Of course you want to be friendly, but not worried. When people sense friendliness without defensiveness, they're more likely to like you for all the right reasons: Because you're nice.

So, whenever you notice your language focusing on something negative, every chance you get, flip the switch, and level up your language by emphasizing the positive side of things.

Chapter 10

TURBO-CHARGING YOUR COFFEE SELF-TALK

Ok. With all the talk of how important it is to make sure your feelings match your great words, thoughts, goals, and dreams, here are four awesome ways to help you amp up your positive energy. I regularly do all of the following, for maximum sparkle and shine.

1. Use Images

Our brains absolutely adore images.

You can make your Coffee Self-Talk more powerful by adding pictures to your self-talk scripts. When you do this, it gets more parts of your brain firing, which helps you feel the elevated emotions *even more.*

Our brains love images because they're more memorable than words, and they turbo-boost your brain's rewiring process. That's why memory experts say the key to remembering things easily is to use mental images. You can do this with pictures from the internet, pictures you take yourself, or even pencil-and-paper sketches or doodles. Think of it like "Coffee Self-Talk Meets Pinterest" or "Coffee Self-Talk Meets Vision Board."

You can use images with every self-talk statement if you like, or only occasionally, for special emphasis. The pictures can relate directly to the statement, but they don't have to. What's most important is that the picture triggers the uplifted emotion you're trying to capture.

For example, for the line, *I am having the most awesome day today!*, you could add a picture right after that statement. Just grab any stock photo you love from the internet. It could be a picture of the ocean, or the mountains, an animal, or art. Anything that inspires awe in you.

My own Coffee Self-Talk has lots of pictures I grab from the internet to inspire me. When I see them, I feel extra power coursing through my veins. The pictures make me feel more electric and amplify my feelings. For example, I have a part of my script where I write about my new self. It says:

I am a new person.
I gave up the old identity, and I'm living a completely new,
magical life of my design. Courageous. Excited. In awe.
In love with life. Patient. Kind. Shimmering Gold.

Then, following the statement is a picture of the mythical phoenix bird burning, transforming, and rising from the ashes.

If you want to be healthy, you could add a picture of something that makes you *feel* healthy. Maybe it's a picture of healthy food. Or people playing a sport. Or running on the beach with a dog. Or maybe it's a girl doing yoga. The point is to find pictures you love that also make you feel elevated emotions. Add those pictures throughout your Coffee Self-Talk to inspire and boost those uplifted feelings.

The experience of seeing these images while doing your Coffee Self-Talk is like reviewing a living, breathing, powered-up vision board (a bulletin board where you put images that inspire you or that depict your goals being reached). When you add pictures and emphasis to your self-talk, and read it aloud while seeing these pictures, the manifestation of your dreams can happen faster. You can practically feel it happening in real time.

Now *that's* powerful!

2. Emojis!

Another fun and quick way to enhance your Coffee Self-Talk is with emojis. My pages of scripts are filled with them. I like the rainbow, the fortune teller's crystal ball, hearts of all colors, smiles, sun, moon, stars, the flexed bicep, dance, coffee (of course), the bag of money, airplane, beach/island, butterfly (as in transformation!), and more. *Get creative.* It's a fun and meaningful process, and you'll find yourself adding to it over time. There's something about the lighthearted playfulness of the designs that engages you at a subtle emotional level. It's as though you're telling yourself, *don't be too serious, and have fun as you kick ass achieving your goals!*

See? Uplifted emotions.

3. Fonts, Underlines, Italics, and Bold

To add emphasis to certain phrases, I underline words, bold, and/or italicize them. I center-align certain statements, right-align others, and change the spacing of the words to add visual variety. I use my iPhone's Notes app to enter my own little scribble drawings, too. All of these make your self-talk more emotionally attention-grabbing, and just plain fun.

4. Say It Out Loud

Some people choose to read their self-talk silently to themselves. Sometimes this might be your only option, such as in a crowded public space. That said, whenever possible, *say your self-talk out loud!*

When you speak your self-talk out loud, you'll be more focused, and your mind will be less likely to wander. It also uses three sensory "modalities":

- Reading (eyes)
- Speaking (mouth)
- Hearing (ears)

Which means it's roughly three times as powerful as reading silently, with respect to the level of activity inside your brain.

Oftentimes, when reading silently, your mind can wander. Such as thinking about your to-do list, or the gossip you heard the other day, or what clothes to wear. By reading, speaking, and hearing your self-talk, it makes your focus laser-sharp. This, in turn, makes the words easier to remember, and it makes them more meaningful, too. Speaking the words also makes them enter your subconscious mind for faster effectiveness, and it helps you connect with a deeper emotional response.

As I've said many times already, it's ok if you don't yet believe the words coming out of your mouth. You can totally *fake it till you make it* because that actually works. The legendary boxer, Muhammad Ali, was famous for doing this. He once said, *"To be a great champion, you must believe you are the best. If you're not, pretend you are."*

Even when you're pretending, your brain is still firing and wiring, because it doesn't know the difference between what you're imagining is happening and what is really happening. You can think of it as "rehearsing for success." Pretty soon, you won't be pretending. It will be real.

And if you can't say your self-talk out loud for whatever reason, at a minimum, mouthing the words silently will have more impact than just reading your Coffee Self-Talk to yourself. At a VERY minimum, have good posture while you're doing this, meaning sit up straight. Trust me on this, it just works. Something about *snapping to attention* and mouthing the words with *intention*—makes your brain take notice. Do a little experiment right now and try this. You'll see what I mean!

5. Act as If

For even more impact, get really *animated* while saying your Coffee Self-Talk. By really emphasizing the words and whooping-n-hollering between statements—*YEAHHH!!!*—you *seriously* amplify your emotional state.

The more action and emphasis you put into this, the better and more believable it will be for your mind and body. So go for the gusto! Tap into your inner movie star. *Act it, baby!* By really getting into it, you carve those affirming self-talk grooves deeper into your brain, and faster.

Your body *will* respond to your words. And if you add glittery sass, energy, and emphasis, the response will be even stronger.

Also effective is to sometimes stand up and say your self-talk in a power pose, like Wonder Woman! Yes, *I actually do this.*

Crazy? Don't care. Hell, I even post pictures of me doing it online. Power poses have been shown to increase confidence and decrease stress, so take advantage of them. Feel silly doing it? No problem, do it anyway. Make a joke of it, if you like. Ham it up. Here's a good one: hands on hips, eyes straight ahead, and a slight, knowing smile. (You know the one, that expression that shows you have the secrets, the power, and the answers.) *Yes! Power up, girl!*

6. Make It Like a Movie by Adding Music

Without music, life would be a mistake.

— FRIEDRICH NIETZSCHE

The next leveling up in Coffee Self-Talk comes when you add powerful music to the mix. It can be playing in the background as you read your self-talk out loud, or mixed into self-talk you record yourself.

Adding music while reading your Coffee Self-Talk will amplify and intensify the feelings you want to create. Music can evoke powerful emotional responses, and it's one of the easiest ways to reduce stress, alter your mood, and change your state *instantly*.

I've mentioned the importance of feelings while reading your Coffee Self-Talk, and an easy way to uplift your emotional state is by listening to uplifting music while you're going through it. There's a reason movies have soundtracks and scores. They drive people's emotions while they watch the movies. Think of one of your favorite dramas or action-packed summer blockbusters, and imagine what it would be like without music! The experience would be so much less moving or memorable. By adding uplifting music, you'll not only take your Coffee Self-Talk to the next level, but you'll also enjoy it more!

Go through your favorite songs, and find one that uplifts your spirit, inspires your soul, and moves you emotionally to feel powerful and energized. Then, put it on repeat, and listen to it while you read your Coffee Self-Talk. Call it your "Coffee Self-Talk song." Or you could compile several songs and create a "Coffee Self-Talk playlist." I like the playlist idea for its variety, but I personally find that repeating just one song, over and over, is most powerful because it anchors that one song very strongly to the scripts I'm reading. In a few months, or even a year, I might move on to a different song, or when entering a new chapter in life.

Pro-tip: Choose a song *without lyrics* so the words don't compete with your focus as you read your Coffee Self-Talk. I find certain movie scores have the perfect epic, dramatic, cinematic feel for this purpose. Or look for some cool, techno tracks with an electric, ambient beat.

7. BONUS! Record Your Coffee Self-Talk

Next up for the superstars is to record yourself speaking your self-talk... *wait for it...* with your chosen song playing in the background! OMG, it's totally fun and fascinating. By recording your self-talk, you can now listen to it at any time. Like walking to school, driving a car, getting ready in the morning, working out at the gym, cooking dinner, doing the dishes, or cleaning your room.

Heck, one of my ultimate favorite ways to do my Coffee Self-Talk is with my coffee mug in hand, while walking around my kitchen and living room with my headphones on, listening to my recorded self speaking into my ears. There's some powerful stuff going on here, making your self-talk more effective because the repetitive motion of walking triggers a profound relaxation response in your body. When this happens, your stress decreases. Simultaneously, you get a boost in energy and an uplifted mood. *Win-Win!*

Remember, uplifted feelings and elevated emotions are key ingredients to having your self-talk and dreams manifest faster. And the rhythmic motion of walking benefits our brains in remarkable ways.

I understand we don't all have time to regularly sit down and read our Coffee Self-Talk every single morning. By recording it, you can listen to it and tap into its greatness on days when you're rushed and drinking your coffee on the go. Or, if you're going all out, it means you can experience your life-changing self-talk more than once a day. Sit down with your Coffee Self-Talk in the morning, as normal, reading it and sipping your coffee. Then, when you're working out or brushing your teeth before bed, play it again in the background.

Hearing your own recorded voice can be a little weird at first. That's normal, and it's always temporary. Like the strangeness of seeing yourself in the mirror with a new hairdo—what seems so unfamiliar at first quickly becomes something you don't even notice. It's the same with hearing your own voice. It's worth going through this adjustment period, because the impact of hearing your own self-talk is super powerful!

When you hear your own voice—especially once you're used to hearing it, and not judging it—it plays like an internal dialog in your mind. Like "you" telling "you" how things are. And when you think about it, this is exactly what happens when we think! We think in dialog—mostly unspoken—with ourselves constantly. "What should I wear today? Hmm, I like this shirt, but I wore it two days ago..." etc.

I like to think of my recorded self-talk as my "higher self"—the part of my brain that knows what's best for me in the long run—and I trust it. When I hear this voice, it has a kind of authority. It's a kind of power, and it comes from me!

Here's how I go about recording my own self-talk:

There's nothing fancy here... no professional audio equipment or anything like that. I'm the only one who's going to hear it, and it doesn't have to be perfect.

As I mentioned, I use the Notes app on my iPhone to type my Coffee Self-Talk. This is very convenient, as my phone is always on me, and so I can add to my self-talk script and make edits any time I get an idea, or the inspiration hits me. I also have an iPad, which syncs with that Note in the cloud. So I pull up my Coffee Self-Talk on the iPad and read it from there. I also have the music playing on my iPad while I'm reading. Then, I open the Voice Memo app that comes pre-installed on the iPhone, though any recording app would work.

I then record my Coffee Self-Talk into my iPhone, while reading it out loud from the iPad, with the music playing in the background on the iPad. The end result blends my voice with the music just fine. This process won't win any awards for its sound quality, but it's more than good enough to reprogram your brain for living your magical life!

If you don't have a separate tablet device to read from, just read your self-talk script from your computer, or print it out on paper. Music isn't necessary, but it's more effective. It's also more fun!

Or, you could always just write your script down on paper, and read from that while you record.

On most days, I listen to my recorded self-talk once a day. Sometimes, I'm feeling extra energized, and I leave it playing on an endless loop, listening on headphones while I go about my business. *It's amazing!*

8. One More Idea: The "I am" Mobile App

There's an app for iPhone/Android that's perfect for using with your daily Coffee Self-Talk. The app is called "I am," and it's billed as "daily affirmations for self-care," by the app developer, Monkey Taps.

The app has a free preview mode where you can sample preloaded affirmations. The full version costs about $20 a year and gives you access to its full library of preloaded affirmations, including a feature that lets you add your own (including emojis, yay!).

And this is where your Coffee Self-Talk comes into play.

Simply add lines from your Coffee Self-Talk script into the app. Click "Practice," select "My Own Affirmations," and choose a time (one, five, or 15 minutes). The app will randomly display your Coffee Self-Talk lines at 15-second intervals, with pretty backgrounds.

So in this way, it creates a timed Coffee Self-Talk session for you, and another cool way to go through your script!

In addition to using the app during your morning Coffee Self-Talk routine, it's also a great way to fill idle time. Just imagine... standing in line with your mom or dad at the grocery store, and you pull out your phone, and the following line from your script appears:

I am a great person, with a big heart, and big smile.

What a super way to inject some good feelings into your day!

Chapter 11

WHAT TO DO AFTER YOUR COFFEE SELF-TALK

Question: What do I do *after* my Coffee Self-Talk?

Answer: Go about your life.

Do you ever love how you can throw some leftovers into the microwave, poke a couple of buttons, and 60 seconds later, it's ready to eat? You don't sit there wondering if it will work this time, or thinking about how it happens (well, unless you're a scientist at heart). You just know the food will come out hot. You simply expect it.

You trust the process.

Same idea applies here. You don't need to get caught up with *how* the thing you want is going to manifest. If you have big, beautiful dreams of going to a great university, or becoming an entrepreneur and changing people's lives, or making millions of dollars, or even just improving your current life situation right now, you might be tempted to think to yourself *how in the heck is it actually going to happen?*

Good News!

I'm here to tell you that you don't need to focus on the *how* it happens. Not yet. You just want to focus on *what you want* and then *think and feel good things about it.*

Why? The reason you don't have to know the *how* right now is because that'll become clearer to you as you do this daily process of Coffee Self-Talk. Remember your Reticular Activating System (RAS) from Chapter 6? If you recall, that's the part of your brain that focuses your attention and filters information from the world around you. Well, as you do your Coffee Self-Talk, recall that your RAS Wizard will start kicking in and doing its thing. In short order, it will seem as though ideas and information are being drawn to you automatically through your new energy and focus, and you'll start seeing these amazing things and opportunities sparkling right before your eyes, because your brain is now trained to see them.

The path will become well-lit, and the steps will become obvious, because they feel so right. Your intuition will weigh in, and you'll know how to move toward your dreams because you'll sense it and feel confident. It'll feel good. It'll be exciting. There will be nudges and urges from inspiration to move or do something. You'll just know what to do... even in those cases when the best decision is to sit tight until you have more information. You'll start to notice opportunities and options. And sometimes, you'll have *so many options!* And other times, you'll find something you're interested in, and you'll start down that path, only to realize it's curving in a wonderful, different way that you didn't expect.

That happened to me. When I first started doing my Coffee Self-Talk, I included lines about becoming a millionaire, living a magical fun life, and all that great stuff. At that time, I thought the path to my dream life would be my husband writing fiction. I imagined him writing amazing thrillers, the kind that get made into movies.

But then, something unexpected happened.

And that is, even though my husband was the fiction guy in our family, remember when I told you back in Chapter 3 that I had added those three lines about creativity and storytelling into my Coffee Self-Talk?

I am a creative genius.
I have tons of stories to tell.
I am a prolific writer.

Well, story ideas started coming to me. *Like magic.* And when the first coronavirus lockdown came, for the hell of it, we both decided to try writing novels... in one month. (There's a cool challenge online that inspired this, called "NaNoWriMo." Google it, if you like to write.)

My husband started writing the first day, dutifully banging out 1500–2000 words a day. I spent the first week outlining and plotting my very first novel, a steamy romance about a mismatched couple locked down together due to the virus. I didn't write a single word of actual book though.

Each day, my husband would ask if I had started writing. "Not yet," I'd say. Day after day. But on the tenth day, I'd done enough planning, and I started to write.

And that's when I discovered that I had a superpower.

Speed.

Like, five thousand words a day. My husband was blown away. I surpassed his total word count in a few days. And then I started doing *ten thousand* words a day. I was a machine. Almost in a trance. As though channeling words from... who knows where.

A few days later, I finished my novel. I didn't know if it was any good. Then my husband read it. And he said we needed to have "a meeting."

Uh-oh. That didn't sound good.

"You're a novelist," he said. "I suggest I stop writing my thriller, switch to editing your romance novels full time, and we publish them as fast as you can write them."

Whoa.

In that minute, both of our careers turned on a dime. Like, in a whole new direction. And over the next eight months, we busted our asses and published *eight* novels.

But that's not where this story ends.

That's when the second unexpected thing happened.

Sometime before I started writing novels, I had nearly finished writing a little, non-fiction self-help book called... wait for it... *Coffee Self-Talk*. We had never published it because we were so busy doing the romance novels instead. During a pause between two of my novels, I revisited it, and decided to finish it. Not only would it not take long, but now, I had a good capstone story to tell, about how I'd used my own Coffee Self-Talk to become a novelist, starting from never having written a word of fiction in my life.

And when I say you don't know how the universe will deliver on your goals and dreams... this is what I'm talking about. It wasn't my husband's writing that would do it.

But... it wasn't my romance novels either. Not yet, anyway.

How did the universe deliver on my goals and dreams? What did it hand to me on gold platter? It was *Coffee Self-Talk*. One day, quite unexpectedly, the book started to sell very well. It quickly became an international bestseller. It's no exaggeration to say that, almost overnight, it changed our lives completely.

I had expected my fiction novels to make me a huge success. But it ended up being a project that I'd started much earlier, and shelved. Well, *hells bells*, I never knew it would be *that* book that catapulted my career!

But guess what...

This is SO common!

If you talk to a handful of very successful people, you'll be surprised how many of them found success doing something they had never dreamed of when they were younger. In fact, they often made their money in ways that *didn't even exist* when they were younger, such as businesses made possible by the internet.

So, you *really* never know where the road will take you. But you *will* be inspired to do certain things, and talk to certain people, learn about different subjects, hobbies, passions to explore, and skills to develop. And when you keep your energy positive and happy, these things will draw your true desires of self-love and happiness and success to you.

This is really good news.

Why?

It means you can relax!

I don't mean you can relax on the couch. I don't mean you won't work... *of course* you'll work. Hard, in fact. But it means you don't have to *worry*. No one can predict the future. While the universe is conspiring to help you, you can *enjoy the ride*.

And there's a feeling you can tap into that will help you during this unfolding of your future. It'll help keep you even more relaxed while manifesting. It's what I call the *Happy Expectancy Feeling*...

The Happy Expectancy Feeling

Have you ever had a Christmas or other holiday when you already knew what gift you were getting? Or do you have an aunt or a grandparent who always sends you a check for your birthday? Well, when you *know* you're going to get this thing, you don't sit there and obsess about it and wonder how or when it's going to arrive. Instead, you just have this happy expectancy that it's coming. You believe because *you know*.

Or imagine you were going to meet a friend for coffee, and you're really looking forward to it. You probably wouldn't worry that your friend wouldn't show up. I mean, assuming your friend is reliable, you wouldn't sit there and think about it *not* happening. And so you make a date with your friend, and you just relax about it, looking forward to it, which is a good energy. You certainly don't fret or obsess about it.

These examples of a coffee date with a friend, or a Christmas or birthday gift you know is coming to you, are times when you experience what I call the *Happy Expectancy Feeling*. And I want you to think about this feeling, and try to recreate it when you're doing your Coffee Self-Talk.

As you do your Coffee Self-Talk every day, chill out and relax with a feeling of happy expectancy that you're drawing your dreams to you. That you're going to smash through your goals. That somehow—one way or another—it's just going to happen, and you're certain about this. You don't always have to know *how*. Again, that will become clear over time. Discovery is a natural part of the journey.

Your path will start to be lit.

The map will unfold, and you will see where "X" marks the spot.

Your job is simply to show up every day and do the work: *Do your Coffee Self-Talk*. Think and feel positive thoughts while you're doing it. And, as often as possible, do this throughout the day... thinking and feeling great.

If you do this regularly, the happy expectancy feeling will become more natural over time. As you start doing this process, you'll experience successes with it, and see for yourself that it works. Sometimes, the results are immediate. Like when you immediately start to feel better about yourself, or about your life, or about a situation. Or as you gain confidence, which might feel weird at first! Soon, you start to experience more happy moments, and you realize that the "knowing" the happiness would arrive was like a premonition... *seeing the future.*

And then big things happen, like manifesting a big dream, or changing your life course, because you suddenly realize you have this amazing passion for something that you decide to go after.

This Happy Expectancy Feeling is the part of the equation that uses your *belief* in the system. It shows your *belief* in the process.

The more you believe in the process, the faster and better the results.

So, after you think of all the things you want (and the new you that you want to become), and you create your scripts to detail this, and you start doing your Coffee Self-Talk every day... that's when you can also relax, chilling out, with your Happy Expectancy vibe.

And guess what? Relaxing while you think about or work toward your goals is a good, positive emotion that helps you stay focused, on track, and actually *create* that reality.

The Ultimate Recap of Part II: Getting What You Want in Life

Bookmark this page!

Step 1 - Identify What You Want

Identify WHAT you want, and use your WHY to make sure it's coming from a positive place in your mind and heart.

For example: If you want to get into a good college... to be a doctor... to impress others... then that desire isn't coming from a positive feeling of self-worth, because you're looking to other people to validate you.

On the other hand, if you want to get into a good college... to be a doctor... because you've always wanted to be a doctor... and it *sounds awesome*, then that is a terrific WHY.

If you want a certain person's loving attention... because you think he or she will solve all of your problems or make you feel better about yourself, then that desire is not coming from a place of self-worth and self-love.

However, if you want to be in a relationship with someone because the person is a great person, and you're a great person, and you know you two would hit it off, then that is coming from a solid sense of self-worth. *Go for it!*

Pro-tip: Your wants, desires, goals, and dreams can change over time. In fact, they usually do! As you learn more, you'll start to see opportunities you didn't know existed, and some of them might be more appealing than the thing you wanted before.

Step 2 - Do Your Coffee Self-Talk Every Day

This step is simply reading (or listening) to your positive self-talk every day. These affirmations include lines about *what you want,* from step one, above. Any good thought that helps you feel or believe that what you want is possible will align your heart and brain to help you focus and draw it to you.

Pro-tip: The more often you think positive thoughts, and feel positive emotions, the faster the process will happen. You'll know it, because *you'll feel like you're on a mission.* That's why doing Coffee Self-Talk daily helps. Because it's *daily.*

You have the power to shift your internal state at any time, and it happens because you will have trained your brain to do this. This is how you attract your future life *intentionally.* On purpose. It doesn't mean you won't ever face challenges, but it does mean that nothing except you can rule your reaction to things. You are still, always, in charge of your thoughts and your feelings.

Step 3 - Take Action

From steps one and two above, you'll start to see more positive things and cool people coming into your life. You'll start to have new ideas and discover new options. You might learn of another university you hadn't considered before, or a great-sounding major to study. Or you might meet a new friend. You might solve a problem at home, or you might come up with a creative idea for a project or hobby. You might discover a new passion. You might even meet the love of your dreams!

And when *all this cool stuff* presents itself to you, because you attracted it with your happy, sizzling energy, and because your brain's Reticular Activating System helped you see it and pay attention to it, you'll be inspired to *take action*.

And when you consistently take action, with the conviction of someone who *already knows* she is going to succeed, the universe will move mountains for you!

You go, girl!

You are going to live the most amazing, magical life EVER!

PART III

SELF-WORTH

I have a lot of awesome things to say that will help you feel super amazing about yourself.

They will make you walk taller, feel lighter, and shine brighter. Life will become so much easier, so listen up!

Chapter 12

THE POWER OF SELF-LOVE

Warning, I might get a bit SHOUTY in this chapter. I have a lot of passion about this topic: self-love. Which, when you boil it down, really amounts to self-*worth*. Which basically means knowing just how amazing you are. Knowing you are born for the desires in your heart. Knowing you are special, and awesome, and have so much to offer the world simply by being you. Knowing you have it in you to push yourself, take risks, and attempt all kinds of awesome stuff. Knowing you are here to play big!

And there might be times that I get EXTRA SHOUTY because I really want you to hear what I'm saying. Sometimes we need a shakin' of our shoulders to get stuff through our heads. And sometimes, even if you think I might be going over the top, if I can plant the seed of an idea in your heart, then I know it will grow over time, and you'll eventually understand why I was so shouty.

Ok! Let's go get some self-love.

The Power of Your Self-Love

It is very cool to want a great life. I don't care how you look or dress, a smiling, happy, kind person who knows her worth will always attract great things. When my brother was in college, he was in a band, and he had long dreadlocks of all different colors. He had tattoos and piercings. He's wicked smart in math, science, and engineering, he has patented several automotive and aerospace products, and he's always attentive in any conversation, actively listening.

Why tell you about my brother? Because if you had seen him on the street back in his college days, based on his appearance, you might have assumed he was a punk, doing nothing with his life. But you know what? My brother, back then, was always smiling, confident, and gave you the best eye contact you'd ever experienced. He drew you in, and it didn't matter if he was dressed in all black with his dreads or in a t-shirt with his tattoos for everyone to see. I used to watch people react to him, and it was awe-inspiring to see how he drew them in with his charisma and attentiveness. His worthiness. *His self-worth.*

Here's the power that comes with the self-worth you're going to cultivate:

- Shining brighter than ever
- Easily knowing the right decision in tough situations
- Feeling so good, and strong, and happy "in your own skin," that you beam and glow
- Soaring, effortless confidence
- Trusting yourself, liking yourself, respecting yourself
- Feeling happiness for other people's success
- And, of course, putting out constant happy vibes, which attract your dreams to you faster
- And so much more!

Your self-worth is like a beaming light shining into the world to light your path. You'll always know where to go because your light guides you. This is great because, whenever you need to make an important decision, or if the world throws a challenge at you, or if people in your life seem to be leading you in the wrong direction, you can simply look inside and discover *your own truth*. It's your self-worth that makes everything ok. Not what everyone else tells you.

YOU HEAR ME, LOVE?

Your powerful self-worth is the rock that makes everything all right. All the time.

Here are some examples of how loving self-worth helps people:

If someone previously caved to peer pressure easily, self-worth helps her stand tall in her decisions.

If someone used to wrestle with low self-esteem, self-worth smooths that road.

If someone used to date people who didn't treat her well, self-worth corrects that BS *reeeeal* fast. Once you value yourself, you won't be willing to give your time or attention to anyone who doesn't value and respect you.

If someone used to have a problem with jealousy and envy, self-worth fixes that.

If someone used to not feel good enough to deserve happiness, self-worth fixes that sh*t.

Self-worth also helps you tap into your greatest power: your intuition. It does this by making you more self-aware. You begin to honestly assess the pros and cons of possible choices. You begin to trust your judgment. You come to value your feelings. And know your truest self.

My own self-worth was instrumental in becoming an author. It allowed me to keep my head up, stay strong and focused, and it gave me the confidence to put my work out there for all the world to see. It makes me comfortable doing interviews and presenting to large groups of people. It also gives me the confidence to say no to things that don't keep my shimmer-shine glowing bright.

My self-worth is strong, now, because I believe in myself. I feel good about what I'm doing. And what I'm writing and creating. And if someone doesn't like my work, that's ok. You know why? *Because I like my work.* My worth is not determined by how others regard my work, or by how others treat me.

I determine my own worth. And I know my worth is astronomical because everything I do comes from a good place, my loving heart.

You determine your own worth.

There's an important reason to build up your self-worth: It gives you the confidence to be YOU. The *you* that glows and gets excited about whatever it is you get lit about. And the world needs YOU TO BE YOU. The world does not need you to be someone else, not your best friend, not your sibling. Because you have so much to offer and share. Your thoughts and opinions *matter.*

If it's not obvious now, it will be in the future. And that future starts *right now.*

The world needs you to be you. I need you to be you. *You need you to be you.*

The Confidence of Not Knowing It All… and Feeling Good About It

About fifteen years ago, when I first started my blog, I used to be extra cautious about my points of view and what I shared. I didn't want to stir things up. I was afraid of what others would say. I was worried about how others would perceive me and my work. I didn't want to engage in debates. It gave me anxiety. Now though? Inspired by the writer, Henry David Thoreau, I do what he did back in the 1800s. I show up and *"give the world a strong dose of myself."* I now tell my story and thoughts about things, without fear. I also know that I don't know everything. And if someone asks a good question, or has a different point of view, my ego is not rattled. I'm not angry, embarrassed, or defensive.

That's because having confidence—*from having a loving self-worth*—means having confidence in my passions, and confidence in knowing that I don't know it all! And never pretending I do.

That's being authentic.

Authenticity brings true freedom.

Now, you might be asking, how do I have such great self-worth? How can someone just magically get her own soaring self-worth? Especially if she's starting from a low point?

Two words:

Self. Talk.

My dear, simple as it may seem, self-worth all starts with the words in your head. That's what this whole book is about. In Chapter 15, there's a script to get you started on building your self-love. It will make your foundation stronger than ever. Read this script over and over during your daily Coffee Self-Talk, and over the next couple of weeks, watch how you start to shine brighter and brighter. That's literally *all you have to do*. But you must do it... the change won't happen unless you do. And you must do it consistently. Like, every day (or nearly every day). If you do, your words will make a world of difference in how you see yourself and how you see the world.

And soon after that, how the world sees you.

The Unexpected Side Benefit of Having a Loving Self-Worth

A funny thing happens when your self-worth and self-esteem start to improve.

First, you learn to stop judging yourself. Or, if you do, it comes from a place of objectively measuring your progress to see if you're improving. It doesn't come from a place of fear or dissatisfaction. There's no emotion, it's just matter-of-fact. And when you stop judging yourself emotionally, an amazing thing happens... you actually stop judging *other people*, too. And when this happens, a new kind of unexpected bliss and happiness starts to blossom in your life.

When you stop judging others, you free yourself.

Your ego recedes into the background. The need to compare yourself to others fades away.

It also opens your heart to loving others. People you never thought you could love, or you never thought you'd want to love. You start to recognize that so many people are in some kind of pain, or operating from a place of fear. Especially difficult people. Their pain is usually what makes them difficult. You start to understand and have compassion for them.

Whom does this benefit?

Oddly enough... you.

Sure, it might benefit others, say, if you express your love, such as by showing them kindness or helping them in some way. But even if you don't express your love, you *feel differently* toward others. Toward the whole world. And this makes you feel all warm and gooshy inside, glowing, full of, well... love. And this is so healthy for your soul and self-esteem, it's impossible to overstate the benefits. Reduced stress, greater happiness, better health, better relationships, better career... even *longer life!*

It took me 40 years to learn how beneficial it is to not judge others. To just observe. Like a photographer taking pictures of animals in the woods. *Click...* and move on.

I wish someone had told me this when I was in high school! It would have made my whole life SO MUCH EASIER.

I remember one day before I had learned this lesson. I was in someone's house, looking at their family pictures. I was smiling at one of the pictures from a recent wedding. But then, something dark happened. I started thinking about the weight of the people in the photo. Now, the good news is, I stopped myself in my tracks as I realized how horrible it was for me to be thinking about their weight. I can now look back on the experience, and I know why I did it.

First, I'm not proud of that moment. But it taught me a valuable lesson. You see, I was judging them... because I constantly judged *myself* about *my own weight*. It was the lens through which I saw the world. A *me-focused* lens. The lens of an out-of-control ego. I used to hold myself to such a ridiculously high standard when it came to fitness that I automatically projected my point of view—my *values*—onto other people. Ack! Bad Kristen! *Stop that! Not cool!*

And so I stopped, right then and there. And I've never done it again.

(Note: It's fine to have values that you impose on others, such as matters of right and wrong. About how they treat you and others. But how they treat themselves? The choices they make for themselves? Well, unless we're very close to them, that's generally none of our business. Don't be too quick to judge... you never know what struggles people may be dealing with.)

The great thing is that, as you start to love yourself—AS YOU ARE RIGHT NOW! —you don't have to wait until you're perfect. Perfection never comes... you just keep getting better and better!

This goes both ways, too. You can use this idea to understand other people *who judge you*. When they're judging you, it's only because it comes from their own point of view about themselves. It's never really about you. (The exception is with people who genuinely care for you, such as teachers—whose job is to prepare you for the world —and parents, and loved ones. They just want to see you happy, and this can cause them to judge you—your decisions and actions, for example—from a place of wanting to protect you, rather than to boost their own egos.)

Loving yourself *as you are now* is super important! Don't wait for the future you. This doesn't mean we don't try to improve our lives, of course. In fact, the desire to improve ourselves and our lives automatically results from building a foundation of self-love!

It's very easy. Every morning, simply say things in your Coffee Self-Talk like,

I love me just as I am today.
I love my body. I love my life.

You'll gradually build a strong foundation of self-love and self-worth, and this will make you less judgy... of you, and the people in your world.

Amazing Life Tip: Entertain Yourself

When I was very young, one of the best skills my mom taught me was to be able to entertain myself. It's one of the best things you can do for yourself—right now, and for the rest of your life.

The concept is super simple. It means you have hobbies and things that you enjoy doing, and they're things that can be done by yourself. For example, tennis would not fit this description. It's a great hobby, but it's not an example of entertaining yourself because it requires another person.

For me, I love to read, both fiction and nonfiction. I love watching movies. I love listening to music. I love writing. And cooking. I love nature and going on walks. If you were to ask my daughter, she'd say that she loves to draw, play her ukulele, knit, and play games on her iPad. All good examples of things that can be done alone.

One of the reasons so many people had a hard time with self-isolation during the COVID-19 pandemic was because they didn't know how to entertain themselves. They were used to relying on other people and things outside themselves to find any joy.

So, think about things *you love to do* that don't require other people, and make sure you set aside some time in your week for some of these pleasures. If you don't have any, then think of things that you'd like to learn to do over the next three months. Explore!

Here's a bonus: Entertaining yourself helps boost your self-esteem.

Huh?

Come again, Kristen?

That's right. Learning to self-entertain will boost your self-esteem, because you'll feel self-reliant, not depending on others to fill the empty spaces in your day or life. At any time, you'll have plenty of things to do that'll spark joy, and it will all come from inside of you. Having more interests means having more options.

And a key to winning in so many situations—including life—is *having options*.

Things to Remember

1. Your Coffee Self-Talk will build your self-worth, and this will change your life.
2. Try not to judge others. Some people are struggling in ways we know nothing about.
3. Learning to entertain yourself helps make you self-reliant and gives you more options.

Chapter 13

SOCIAL MEDIA

I typically use really positive language about pretty much everything. I love finding the silver linings in bad situations. It's almost a game to me.

But, I gotta say... social media is a real mixed bag.

On one hand, it can be absolutely wonderful. Such as teaching you about stuff you never would have heard about otherwise, or allowing you to stay in touch with friends, over the course of your whole life, no matter where they live, anywhere in the world.

But on the other hand... well, social media has a dark side.

It's one of the biggest problems of our times. For too many women, it can be a soul-destroying, toxic cesspool. And a terrible way to spend your time—if you're not doing it wisely. I was once a victim of this myself. It's as though social media was custom built to make us feel inadequate. To compare ourselves to one another, and question whether we're good enough, or pretty enough, or rich enough, or cool enough... simply by having us obsess all day long, looking at an artificial, glam-filtered, Photoshopped view of what's going on in everyone else's life. And let's be honest... people are always showcasing their best-of-the-best pics.

But that's only part of the problem with social media.

The other major issue is the nasty energy that can be out there. It sucks, but some people are just way too comfortable spewing ugliness from the safety of being behind a screen. It cracks me up though, as most of them would never say these things to someone's face!

What makes people be so mean?

Simple. They lack self-love. People who love themselves have no desire to bring other people down. In fact, they try to lift others up!

And while reading crappy comments from people who lack self-love is no fun... well, I'm going to say something that might seem weird. (Though, if you're this far into the book, it will just seem like normal Kristen.) When you're doing your Coffee Self-Talk program, and you're radiating buckets of good feels and vibes, you might actually find less trash-talk on your feed, because your vibe doesn't match theirs, and so they're not even mentally where you are, as though you're on a different planet. And if they continue being negative or nasty, and you just don't respond, because you don't care, and you just keep on shining, they quickly realize their efforts are a waste of time, and they'll move on to stir things up with people who are easier to get a reaction from.

Is this 100% guaranteed? No, but it's a general, good consequence that follows naturally from the sparkly energy you're putting out into the world. So that's the good news! Like I said though, there are still some people, for whatever reason, trying to bring down your energy to their level because they're unhappy, and they don't want to be unhappy alone. Don't fall for their trickery! You know better, especially after reading this book. Your happy energy is what is going to give you the happiest life.

And of course, if someone is a constant source of negativity, consider disconnecting from them. This isn't always possible, such as with family members, but for the most part, you can choose which people you associate with.

And finally—I'm saving the big guns for last, here—the *really* effective way to minimize negativity from social media is simply not to spend much time there in the first place. Like, limit it to fifteen minutes a day. Or ten. Or ten minutes every other day. I promise, the world will keep spinning without you checking in every half hour, like a lab rat in a cage, clicking a button for a food pellet. (Sorry to get all dark here, but the social networks literally experiment on you to find out how to keep you addicted, so you'll see more ads, and make them more money.) I can't tell you how many people have told me that, when they slashed their time on social media, their heart felt lighter, and they became so much happier.

I mean, it's not that complicated. If social media is a toxic stew... *get out of the damn stew!*

But if you still want to spend time on there, then BE SMART ABOUT IT! Look for people to follow, and vibe with, who have the same good energy as you. I love following high-vibe accounts, like cheerful people who post uplifting pics about nature, travel, and other positive peeps drinking the same positive-energy Kool-Aid as me. They can actually be inspiring! And when you're super particular about whom you pay attention to, you're not a servant to social media, *you're its master.*

I take the same, strict, no-BS approach to ALL of my social media feeds. Several years ago, I wasted far too much time on social media. When I realized these gamified platforms were manipulating me, putting me into a constant mode of addicted consumption, I said, "*Aww, hell no.*"

I made some major changes.

For starters, I didn't like all the smack-talk on Twitter, so I immediately stopped following *anyone* who was more often negative than positive. It didn't matter if we were personal friends or not. I refuse to hold my consciousness hostage to the consciousness of negative or petty people. Imagine if everyone unfollowed negative people so ruthlessly... Twitter would quickly become a much friendlier place.

Come to think of it, so would the world.

Instagram was another constant source of distress. Because of my own self-esteem issues, I found too much *comparisonitis* going on in my head—constantly gauging whether my life was keeping up with others—and it never put me into an uplifted state. Sadly, this is common for many people using Instagram today. When one's self-esteem is low, getting on Instagram, where people only post their best, photo-filtered selves, it can make for a wicked cauldron of toxicity to drink.

But there is an answer for this! Social media can be powerful if used correctly, and detrimental if used incorrectly. Here's how I made it a more powerful force in my life, supporting my well-being...

For a long while, I simply cut off social media, cold turkey. I literally deleted those apps from my phone. I did this to add "strategic friction"—like shopaholics who control their impulsivity by freezing their credit cards in a block of ice in the freezer. They can still get to their card in an emergency, but it's a pain in the ass. On purpose.

If I wanted to check-in or post something, I would literally need to reinstall the app, find my password, and log in. Which I did, from time to time. But only if it was important enough to justify the pain-in-the-ass effort required. And when I was done, I would delete the app again. Sounds a little nutty, I know. But this broke my addiction to likes, reposts, and followers.

It was 100% successful.

At first, my days seemed strangely quiet. Not boring (I had plenty to do) but just... what's the word? Ah... *peaceful*. It was like after you've become used to some sound, and you're no longer aware of it, like a fan with a slight buzz, and then it turns off, and the silence sounds wonderful, but you hadn't realized it had been bugging you slightly, until it was gone. Well, the day I removed these apps, it was like a busy New York City street scene—with taxis honking and sirens—it's like it just faded away and was replaced by a beautiful, wooded meadow, with birds chirping and butterflies. The mental "silence" of not checking in on the world was soooo relaxing. And all my friends and not-really-friends did just fine without me.

But most of all...

It allowed me to take a breath and work on myself.

While I stayed off social media, I was simultaneously working on me, diving into my Coffee Self-Talk. It boosted my self-esteem, and my self-love work made me start to feel *super* worthy. I mean, I started to feel freakin' amazing!

And, as I morphed into a new person, one who felt strong, loving, and confident, I found that I was now in a much better frame of mind for engaging in formerly risky behaviors like browsing Instagram.

Once I felt comfortable getting back into social media, I conducted a ruthless purge. And I mean *ruthless*... as in *Red Wedding-ruthless*, for you *Game of Thrones* fans. Ok, not really, but you get the idea... I unfollowed anybody on any platform that gave me even an ounce of negativity. If people made inappropriate jokes or said mean things about anybody, they were gone. *Adios, muchachos.*

Did I find myself alone, in a deserted social media wasteland? Not at all. Instead, I started following people who made me laugh or had generally positive things to say. I follow leaders in the self-development field, people posting beautiful pictures of animals and nature, and funny people. There are tons of them.

As a rule, I also strictly limit my time on social media—even with my newfound positive friends. There's just no denying that most time spent on social media is simply not productive. It's mind-numbing in a lot of cases, and that's not epic living.

I want to create more than consume!

I want to explore!

I want to learn new things!

I want to work hard on something I love!

I want to play!

So, I get on social for only about five minutes a day. And often, it's only every other day. I even set a five-minute timer on my phone! With all the time I gain not using social media, I spend it making myself and my life better. I walk, I read, I write, I play with my daughter, I meditate, I daydream, I get up and move around, I dance, and I relax—knowing that I'm not wasting a minute, because this is all "bonus" time that's been reclaimed for magical living.

Most importantly, every time I log into Instagram or Twitter (or in your case, perhaps it's Snapchat, TikTok, or whatever comes next by the time you read this), I ask myself one simple question:

Does this make me feel good?

If not, I get the hell out of there. Immediately.

By intentionally keeping as much negativity out of my life as I can, my spirit shines brighter.

I wouldn't have it any other way.

Things to Remember

1. Spend less time on social media. I *promise with all my heart* that you'll feel so much better overall, in life, and you'll be

spending the time doing something that you actually do enjoy, like reading, writing, creating, exercising, hanging with friends, or leveling up with new skills (see Chapter 16's section on Radical Skills Acquisition).

2. When you are on social media, make it time well-spent, and actively seek things that inspire you, and ruthlessly filter out things that don't. Here's the quick test: When you're looking at a picture on Instagram (etc.), if it, IN ANY WAY, makes you feel worse about yourself or your life, then get out of there! Sometimes, you'll simply bail. Other times, it might mean no longer following someone. And other times, there's nothing inherently wrong with the picture, but it makes you feel bad because your self-esteem could be higher. In which case, it's simply a matter of improving your own self-esteem, and later on, you'll feel fine, or even better, seeing pictures like that. For example, a picture of someone in great shape could be either motivating or demotivating—regardless of what shape you're in—based on your own level of self-esteem.

PART IV
COFFEE SELF-TALK SCRIPTS

Now is your time to shine.

You know the key to the magical kingdom. Now it's time to use it.

In Part I, you learned how self-talk works and why it's so amazing. In Part II, you learned how to write your own awesome Coffee Self-Talk, and how to actually *do* your Coffee Self-Talk.

This part of the book provides you with actual scripts to get you started. You can use them right away, as is, or you can pick and choose just the lines you like. Or you can edit them to fit your personal style or situation. And of course, you can always write your own scripts from scratch. I encourage that, but it's something you can work your way up to, using these premade scripts as examples.

Each of these sample scripts dives into a different aspect of your life and shows how Coffee Self-Talk can help in that area.

We begin with a general-purpose script on happiness. Because, hey, if you're happy... everything else is just a bonus, right?

Immediately following the happiness script is an extremely important, foundational script that deals with self-worth. As you'll recall from Chapter 12, self-worth is super important because everything else you do in life will come from your sense of self-worth and self-love. And I mean EVERYTHING!

Beyond these, you'll also see scripts for:

- Your dazzling future
- Academic badassery
- Relationships (friends, family, romance)
- Beauty and body, and
- Dealing with anxiety

And I'll wrap things up with some suggestions about what to do during those times when you're not feeling your sparkliest, whether you're feeling down, or just having an "OOOF" day... you know, one of those days where nothing seems to go right.

Are you ready?

Ok, let's go!

Chapter 14

SPARKLING HAPPINESS

What is a happy life?

It's a life that feels expansive, sparkly, and has amazing, happy surprises that pop up around every corner. It's waking up jazzed, curious, and bright. It has you living in a nearly constant state of wonder and awe, noticing more textures and brilliant colors everywhere you look. It's smiling more because you *can't help it.*

A happy, magical life is a state of mind, and the script in this chapter will help get you into that mindset. The more you read it, the more you say this script out loud, and the stronger you feel it, the more *real* it becomes. Anyone can tap into this source of magic, and when you do, watch out, because *life gets really fun.*

But first...

8 Awesome Rainbow Tips for Happy Living

There are a few simple ways to bring more happiness into your life. Think of it like laying your *happiness foundation*, brick by happy brick. These behaviors automatically set you up for happiness.

1. Honesty

Honesty is *always* going to be a smart policy, because of how it's going to make you feel inside. When you're honest and forthcoming with someone (friends, parents, family, classmates, coworkers, strangers), you feel empowered, and it boosts your confidence. Yes, seriously! And of course, it makes other people trust you. Which, *wait for it...* *also* boosts your confidence.

When in doubt, go the honest route.

2. Promises Kept

Keeping promises—to yourself and to others—is instrumental in helping you live a happy, rainbow-magical life. Just like honesty, keeping promises gives you confidence in yourself, as well as making other people have confidence in you. When you keep promises to yourself, you actually *gain momentum.* Every dream, plan, and goal you set will be fueled by the previous promises you made and kept in your life. You will have a track record of following through. And you'll know it! Meaning you'll have faith in your ability to keep on following through. Start now, start small, and build this stellar track record over time.

3. Forgiveness

Here's one of the most important lessons there is in life: When you don't forgive somebody, whether they know it or not, it's *you who are harmed.*

Huh? Why me?

Because, when you don't forgive someone, you'll carry all that negative energy with you. In fact, they might go on with their lives, probably not even bothered by whether or not you forgive them. But when you do forgive them (even just silently, to yourself), *you set your own soul free.* You unlock your own rainbows. When you forgive, it's telling yourself that your happiness isn't dependent on someone else, or their silly actions! *This empowers you.* It feels amazing.

This means that, no matter what others do, you can be happy. This is a key for living a magical life.

And most of all, *always forgive yourself* when you've made a mistake. Everyone makes mistakes. Myself included. Frequently. But you don't let it get you down. You don't kick yourself. Don't burden yourself with countless "what if" thoughts that do no good whatsoever. Instead, you simply learn from the mistake, and then you let it go and move on.

This process becomes easier as your self-worth and self-love grow, which comes from your self-talk. If you find it difficult to forgive (others or yourself), then add something about forgiveness to your Coffee Self-Talk script. Such as:

> *I love to forgive. Forgiving is healing.*
> *Forgiving always makes my life better.*

And it will.

4. Leaving a Place Better Than You Found It

One of my favorite magical-living tips is to always leave a place better than how I found it. If you're in a bathroom, and there's a dookie in the toilet, then flush it. If you see an empty soda can on the ground, pick it up and throw it away. At home, if you see something that needs to be done, do it. Dishes in the sink? Put them in the dishwasher or wash them.

When you do things like this, it *feeeels* good. Literally, because of brain science. Your brain secretes feel-good chemicals when you do helpful things that nobody told you to do.

And, of course, doing this makes you feel like a good person, because you are! And you attract more amazing things to your life.

There's a word that describes people who do this kind of thing: *Conscientious*.

Conscientious people are more *aware* than others. They pay attention. They notice more when things are wrong. They're thoughtful. Considerate. They not only return their shopping cart to the corral, they sometimes return someone else's, too!

And what do you get for being conscientious? Aside from the exercise from returning all those carts?

You get a strong sense of self-worth.

And that's not all: *You also become successful.*

You see, when people do these little acts of helpfulness, over time, it turns into a habit. And that habit plays out in other areas of your life, like paying attention to the quality of your work. Which means conscientious people do better work, they get better jobs, better projects, and better promotions. This trait is so important that psychologists call "Conscientiousness" one of the "Big Five" personality traits. It's associated with being diligent and organized. And of all the Big Five traits, it's the most predictive of long-term success.

So make your bed, dammit! :)

5. Paying It Forward

Has anyone ever shown you kindness? There are a lot of people out there who could really just use someone being kind to them today. Let that kind person be you. When you pay it forward, it eventually comes back to you.

It makes the world a better place.

But here's something you might not know. *Altruism*, which means helping others, actually causes your brain to secrete feel-good chemicals. This effect is called the "helper's high" because you sometimes experience a rush of feeling good after doing good deeds. So when you're wanting to feel better, so that you can attract a better life, consider helping another person. Your brain and body like this, and, as a reward, they make you feel good.

6. Rose-Colored Glasses

The expression, "seeing the world through rose-colored glasses," means to view the world optimistically, or seeing the good in a situation. Some people criticize optimism as being naïve or blind to the harsh realities of life. Well, I say *hell with that!* Without optimism, humans would still be rubbing sticks together in a cave. The human spirit is amazing! Look how far we've come!

The truth is, we have no problem seeing the hard stuff in life. A problem is obvious. What is *not* always obvious, is the solution. The opportunity. Opportunities *always* exist! We just need to be on the constant lookout for them. And noticing when things go *right*. And being grateful for what we've got.

This is where the rose-colored glasses come in. When you put them on (in your imagination), you are choosing to filter out the negative around you, so that you can see all of the positive. And it really is all around you. You just need to train yourself to notice it.

No doubt, we sometimes find ourselves in difficult situations. Fortunately, there's an easy way we can make every one of them better. It's an example of how you can use positive thoughts to make your life better. The trick is to develop the skill of being able to immediately find something good about *any situation*. Once you get the hang of it, it's easy. I've programmed my mind so it's the default, meaning I automatically look for the good without even thinking about it, or deciding to do it. And you will, too.

Don your rose-colored glasses, baby!

Here's an example... if I'm looking at a building, and there's graffiti on it, decreasing its appeal, I look for something I *do* like about it. Maybe the windows or the door of the building. Maybe the way the sun reflects off it. Even the graffiti itself... I'm reminded of the cave paintings of Lascaux, where humans drew amazing pictures *seventeen freakin' thousand years ago!* The burning desire to make art is in our DNA! And through this lens, I see the graffiti in a different light, and it's beautiful.

Whatever positive thing you come up with, go with that. Anything positive will suffice, and your brain will believe you (it does that), making you feel better instantly.

Or if it's cold, and my hands are freezing while I'm walking to the store, instead of whining, I immediately remind myself that experiencing cold once in a while triggers my longevity genes to express themselves. That's a great thing because I'm going to live a long time! *Woohoo*—thank you, cold weather!

If I have lost something, instead of freaking out, I say, "Well, I just made room for something even better to come into my life."

The bottom line is that you have, available to you at any time, a different perspective on any situation. You'll profoundly improve your life if you can train your brain to always ask the question, *"How else can I view this?"*

This could apply to anything: having rain on your wedding day, or losing your luggage, or spilling ketchup on your white shirt. Or even something big, like a sad breakup, or receiving bad news. Use this approach for anything, and you'll find another way to see the situation. It lifts your spirits. It helps you attract your dreams and live a happier life.

7. The Enjoyment Sniff Test

Start using the enjoyment sniff test. What's that? Imagine an adorable, fluffy Golden Retriever puppy who always sniffs things before she decides to eat it, or chew on it, or play with it. She sniffs it first to see if she'll enjoy it.

Here's how you can use this. For elective things (things you don't *have* to do, like watching TV, or social media) always ask yourself... *Am I enjoying this?* Like, are you *really* enjoying it? *Does it make you feel good?*

Whether it's a song I'm listening to, a movie I'm watching, or a TV show, or scrolling on Instagram, or food I'm eating... is it *feeling* good to do? If not, then I stop. I choose something else instead. This probably seems obvious, but the crazy thing is that, so many times, we do things we don't truly enjoy. Why? Because we're creatures of habit. Got ten minutes before my ride shows up? Whip out the phone, right? Without even thinking. And it's during these moments of not thinking—*not sniffing*, like the dog—that we miss an opportunity to tap into shimmery, elevated emotions.

I recently had a moment of down time, the kind of gap in your day when it seems so normal to "check in" online. But first, I applied the sniff test. Will this bring me joy? And in that moment, I exercised my free will. Instead of following some habit like a robot, I tried to think of a song I hadn't heard in years. I pulled it up on my phone, closed my eyes, and listened to it. The song took me back to when I was a little girl, and nearly brought tears of joy as the memories came back. And in a few minutes, the song was over, and so was my little moment of magic. I returned to my day, with a warm glow in my heart that hadn't been there just a few moments ago.

That's the power of the sniff test.

8. Say No to Clickbait

I don't watch the news regularly—hardly ever, in fact. I don't feel like an uninformed idiot, either. Nowadays, most of the news is either redundant, not important, not relevant, biased opinion, or purely speculative (meaning they have no idea what's going to happen, and they're just filling time talking about "what if?"). Some of it's not even true, and much of what is true is filtered in such a way to make people click, through sensational or scary headlines. Honestly, today's media situation is pretty messed up.

Yet I never seem to miss out when something actually important happens. Big headlines make it through my filter. And nichey stuff that's relevant to my personal interests comes to me via trusted sources. When something is so vital that I must know about it, I dive in to learn more. I don't live under a rock, after all.

But I tell you, when I turned off the news, my mental clarity, mindset, creativity, peace, and happiness skyrocketed. I was freed from SO MUCH daily distraction! There's a saying in the news, "If it bleeds, it leads." This refers to the news industry's incentive to get people to watch by showing them violence, shocking images, and other scary things. Why do they do it? To make you keep watching so you'll watch more ads. In other words, to make money.

Seeing this crap, day after day, is bad for you.

I'm not saying that bad things don't happen in the world, or that you shouldn't know about them. But when you see only bad news, and it's not balanced with good news, your brain forms incorrect intuitions about reality. You're only seeing part of the picture. You're missing all of the examples of wonderful people doing wonderful things and helping one another. Your whole worldview ends up being wrong. And very dark.

The vast majority of the news is negative *because most people are motivated by fear, and they literally can't resist clicking and watching.*

Well, not me. I don't make space for that nonsense in my life. I'm too protective of my uplifted state. I'm fierce about manifesting my happy life, and I'll be damned if I'm going to delay that even one day because some random person did something outrageous in a restaurant and somebody else captured it on video. Call me when war breaks out, or we discover alien life, ya know?

Anyway. Be mindful of the inputs into your brain. Everything you watch, hear, read… *it all affects you.* When you see something on the news, or a headline grabs your attention, before watching it, ask yourself, *Will this help me?* Or, *Do I need to know about this?* You'll find that sometimes it will, and other times it won't. Make the decision with intention.

And now, the fun part... *actual Coffee Self-Talk scripts!*

Coffee Self-Talk Script: My Happiness

I shimmer, and I sparkle, from the moment I awake. My eyes twinkle, and I love my day.

I am magnificent. I am magical. I am happy.

Happiness is all around me and inside me, and I am aligned with my dreams.

I feel like the sun is shining on me everywhere I go, and it reflects a radiance brighter than anything I've known.

I believe in me. I just open my heart and connect to everything happy coming my way.

I'm receiving everything in the dream life I design, because I'm worthy.

My life is amazing, and exciting things happen all the time.

I feel unlimited generosity and patience with myself and others.

Happy, new experiences are coming to me right now.

I'm powerful and capable of doing anything I want. I go after it!

I love doing new things.

My color shines and lights up my life and the lives of others.

I have abundant opportunities all around me. I am creative and having fun with my life.

My needs will always be met. I am open to receive.

I feel like I'm on a scarlet magic carpet ride soaring through a star-bursting sky, filled with awe and wonder.

I'm free as a bird, ready to take flight because my kind heart is expansive and full of love.

I love being generous with others because it makes the world a better place.

The happiness I am seeking also seeks ME.

My imagination runs wild, because I'm filled with creativity.

I am ready to accept miracles! I am ready for happiness. I am worthy of all my heart's desires.

I put out happy vibes day and night, and this attracts my dream life.

I'm in awe of nature and the world around me.

I am worthy of all the happiness in the world.

I focus on choices that excite me.

I am so happy that I feel like I'm walking around in a magical cloud of pixie dust.

When I'm happy... I feel like I have wings. I feel free, light, calm, patient, and relaxed. I feel smiles all around.

I'm here, now, and ready to welcome the happy magic into my life.

Chapter 15

SELF-LOVE

Part III of this book was all about self-love and self-worth, so I won't introduce the topic here, except to say that this is one of the most important scripts you'll ever use if you have any doubts—big or small —about whether or not you *deserve to have a happy life*.

Let me just say this... if you are alive, then you deserve to have a happy life.

We all do.

It is 100% normal to have something that you don't like about yourself, or that you'd like to improve. And that's *fine*. In fact, we should *all* be trying to always improve ourselves. It is not only possible to love yourself while you work on it, but loving yourself *is required*. Because, if you don't first love yourself, then you won't think you deserve to improve, and you won't try.

The first step is simply to *love yourself fully*. Love who you are, and the woman you are becoming, with all your heart. If this feels right and natural, excellent! If you find yourself resisting it, don't worry, that's very common during the teen years, as people transition from children into adults. It can be a confusing and disorienting process. But I promise you, if you read the following script, every day with your delicious cup of coffee, you'll be loving yourself completely in no time.

And then, just watch how the magic starts to unfold!

Coffee Self-Talk Script for Loving Self-Worth

I am worthy of love.

I am worthy of tons and tons of love. Buckets full of love.

I am a great creator, and I like to explore.

Loving myself is fun, and my life gets better each day I love myself.

I have fun playing, laughing, and being myself. I like me.

I have a world of opportunities out there for me. I am excited about life.

I can do anything I put my heart and mind into. It's a wonderful feeling.

I like doing nice things for people because it feels good.

I am a nice person, and I feel this niceness inside of me all day long.

I am a good person. I sparkle, shimmer, and shine.

I am considerate of others, and I am worthy of kindness from others. We all are.

I feel love with my heart, moment by moment, and I have a bright, smiling attitude.

I am my own cheerleader. Go, me, go!

I'm living a completely new life of my own creative design.

I am full of glittering happiness. My energy brings good into my life, because I feel good.

I am confident, and I shine like a star. I am thankful for my life.

I take care of myself by focusing my mind, because I'm worthy. I am so very, very worthy.

I like helping others. Yes! It feels amazing!

I like myself because I'm super likable. I'm kind. I'm fun.

I like taking care of my body because it keeps me healthy and strong.

I like doing new things because it's exciting.

I am worthy of love and respect.

I am in charge of my focus, and I choose to see the positive. It's my choice and my responsibility.

I am kind and compassionate with myself. When I love myself, my eyes sparkle, and I shine.

I am smart, and I love to learn.

I can achieve because I'm capable and focused. I rock!

Chapter 16

YOUR DAZZLING FUTURE

Here's to Your Future Success!

This Coffee Self-Talk script is for those days when you ponder your future, thinking about longer-term goals, like after high school. The reason to start this, *today*, is to draw these dreams to you faster by putting out the right energy *now*. Also, because it's exciting!

Before we get to the script about your awesome, dazzling future, I want to share with you three pro-tips that'll change your life. They have the power to make you extremely valuable to employers (and others) in the future. And being valuable doesn't just mean you'll have more security and money (which it does), but it also promises to give you something even *more powerful*...

Options.

When you have options—such as where to work, what kind of work you do, where to live, how you spend your time, and so on—that's where true, long-term satisfaction comes from.

Whenever faced with a difficult decision, if you don't know what to do, you'll almost never go wrong by choosing the path that will give you the most options down the road.

Tip #1 - Pick Teachers in College

In high school, you don't always have a lot of control over which teachers you get. But if you're college-bound, you'll often be able to choose your teachers. This is one of the best tips I've *ever received. Ever! Ever! Ever!...*

Pick the teacher, more so than the class.

That's because, when you're learning about something from an amazing, cool, talented teacher, you'll learn so much more because the class is more engaging, interesting, inspiring, and fun. All because of the teacher. If there's a class you want to take, but the teacher is lousy, or if he or she isn't passionate about the subject, you won't get as much out of the class. In fact, you may end up not liking the subject you thought you liked *just because of how it was taught!*

The flip side is also true: Sometimes, a great teacher will make you fall in love with a subject that you previously had no interest in!

Think about that...

One great teacher could potentially set you on a whole new life trajectory, pursuing something you're absolutely passionate about, that you currently don't even know exists.

Now, I'm not suggesting you switch majors because of one teacher with a bad reputation, and it's a required class for your major. Sometimes, you just have to power through it. But, in general, if you pick the teacher over the class, or if you pick the great teacher even though it's during some criminal time slot like 7:00 AM (*eek!*), or if you have a choice between a few similar electives (such as if you need a science credit, and you get to choose from a variety of science topics), then picking the class based on the teacher can make a huge difference.

To help you decide, consider what other students say about teachers... factor all of that into your decision. And if you find a teacher you love, you might want to take more of his or her classes.

One last thing about teachers: Most students try to avoid teachers with a reputation for being "hard." That's understandable. But in my experience, the hard teachers were *always the best*. They weren't hard because they were mean. They were hard because they demanded excellence from their students. When you demand excellence from yourself, you'll discover that these teachers are the best teachers in the world.

Tip #2 - Identify Your Dream Job

Some people know, from a very early age, what they want to do when they grow up. These people always amazed me for their foresight... though, if I recall, they all wanted to be either doctors or firemen. Or Batman. Basically, something they saw on TV. Or maybe something one of their parents did for a living.

Which is fine. But it makes you wonder... when they chose their future calling, did they really know much about the range of options?

Funny story. When my husband was in high school, the guidance counselor had everybody take a career assessment thingy. Basically, you answer some questions, and the form magically tells you what you should do for a living. Well, my husband had mentioned in the questionnaire that he liked hiking, and the form told him that he should be... wait for it... *a forest ranger*.

As he tells it, the discussion afterward with his counselor went something like this:

My husband: You mean, like Smokey the Bear?

Counselor: You indicated that you like spending time outdoors. A career in the outdoors might make you happy.

My husband: A lot of money would make me happy. Do forest rangers make a lot of money?

Counselor: Well...

My husband: I want to be an import/export broker. What should I have answered on the questionnaire to make it recommend that?

Counselor (looking down at the form): I don't think that was one of the options...

(Apologies to any guidance counselors out there... my husband's counselor was fantastic. This was the '80s, and the pre-internet assessment tools were not as good as they are today.)

If you look carefully, you may notice a similarity between young people wanting to be forest rangers, doctors, or Batman when they grow up:

Their options are limited by what they know exists.

(Ok, Batman doesn't actually exist. Probably.)

In other words, *exposure*. You can only imagine being in a career to which you've been exposed. Which makes sense, right? I mean, how can you want to be something you don't know exists?

Problem is, most teens haven't been exposed to 99% of the actual jobs out there. Which leads many people down the wrong path, pursuing some career that they find out—sometimes, too late—that they don't like.

Or they just do what their parents did, because it's familiar. Or maybe they do what their parents urge them to do.

Or... maybe the most common of all... they end up in a career related to the first real job they happened to get. Which sometimes turns out great. But you have to wonder, what if, by sheer chance, they'd gotten a different first job? Would they have ended up in a whole different career? Maybe one they like ten times more?

It's a little scary, the idea that your whole future might hinge on mere chance, like the flip of a coin. Fortunately, there's a solution. A way to avoid the problem of falling into the wrong career because you didn't know other options existed.

First, unless you're already really passionate about a certain career (it does happen sometimes, in a good way), don't feel pressure to decide now.

Second, without necessarily deciding now what you want to do later, *do* try to *keep your options open*. (Remember what I said about options in Chapter 12? You always want options.)

Frankly, there aren't many decisions you can make in high school that will permanently close the door to possible future career paths. For instance, if science is your thing, and you get a bachelor's degree in microbiology, there is absolutely nothing to prevent you from going to law school after you graduate from college. In fact, that's a pretty badass combo, and there are probably plenty of jobs for lawyers who have a background in microbiology.

But when I say that decisions in high school won't close off future options, there are a few important exceptions:

Math, Science, and Technology

While it is possible to start down a non-technical path, with weak math, science, and tech skills (especially programming), and transition later into a career requiring these... it can be very difficult. You would be competing against people who've been doing it since high school, and these skills build in such a way that it's hard to catch up, unless you're very motivated or naturally talented.

If there is *any chance whatsoever* that you might one day desire a career that requires any of these skills—even if you don't know which field it is yet—then the best way to keep your options open is to beef up these skills as much as you can, such as taking more of these classes than are required to graduate from high school. Even if you end up in a non-technical field, you'd be surprised how useful these skills can be, both professionally as well as in your personal life.

Solid STEM skills are also a great backup. Remember my musician brother with the dreadlocks? His band was quite successful, but when he became a father, his life of playing gigs on the road came to an end. It was his engineering degree that allowed him to raise a family.

Sports
Compared to other vocations, most athletes have a very short window for their career. There are exceptions, but most pro athletes got a start in their sport pretty young.

Music
People can learn to play any instrument at any age, but the opportunities for college scholarships in music are competitive, and therefore favor those who've been practicing the hardest for the longest time.

(With one possible exception: The viola. It's a string instrument, bigger than a violin but smaller than a cello. In some regions, the college orchestras have a shortage of students who play it. Which means students who play the viola have a good chance of getting a scholarship to these schools. You should confirm whether this is true at your target schools, but what an awesome way to pay for college, right?)

Third, when you're thinking about what you want to do for a

career, I want you to expand your thinking, and imagine that a universe of possibilities exist beyond your current vision... *because it does*. Tap into all of your hobbies, and all your passions, and all the things you love spending your time on, and consider them when thinking about your career. Do you like travel? Coding? Art? Sports? Writing? Video games? Chemistry? Lego? Cooking? Cosplay? Shopping? Fashion? For anything you think of, there's somebody who has figured out a way to make a rewarding career out of it!

Why is passion important for choosing a career? Well, you're probably thinking that it's important because the job will be more interesting. And that is true. But there's another reason. The job market is competitive. Whatever field you enter, the best way to do it is to be focused on becoming *very good at it*. When you love a topic, becoming good at it is fun and rewarding. If you don't, not only is it not fun, but it's also unlikely that you'll become as good at it as the people who love doing it. Why? Because they're spending more time and energy on it, because they enjoy it.

I once asked a family member, a high school senior, if she knew what she wanted to do after college. "Become a lawyer, I guess," she said. The *I guess* says it all, right? I probed deeper...

> Me: What's the Sixth Amendment?

> Her: I don't know.

> Me: I don't either. But in law school, you're going to be competing with people who've known that since eighth grade. Don't go to law school if you're not *fascinated* by law. You either need to *become* interested in it, or find something *else* you're interested in.

Be bold and explore all ideas. You might not know how you'll become something... maybe you want to be a pilot, or a screenwriter, or an inventor, or an entrepreneur, and you think, *how in the heck is that going to happen?*

But remember, your thoughts, your focus, your energy, your inspired action... they can make it all happen. So your job is to focus on those things you love, and let life's flow and your sparkly, resourceful brain guide you. Nothing is off limits when you train your energy and focus on it.

Remember, with zero formal training or experience, I became a novelist in almost no time at all. And, while certain professions require years of specialized training (doctors, accountants, engineers, etc.), there are so many learning resources available to you online *now* that let you learn almost anything about any career before you decide to formally study it.

This is something new! It was not available to your parents. The room for exploration is virtually infinite, limited only by your imagination and curiosity.

Fourth, once you've identified some areas that look potentially interesting, you want to find out more about them.

But there's a problem when you're first learning about something:

You don't know what you don't know.

College is good for this, because they introduce you to everything you'll initially need to know about that topic.

But when you're researching things on your own, it's hard to know where to start. In the past, I would have pointed people to the library to check out books on the subject. And that's still a great option. But nowadays, with all of the amazing free content out there, I'd tell people to start in two other places:

1. YouTube
Simply go to YouTube, and type in questions such as the

following, inserting your area of interest instead of the examples I use:

What's it like to be a martial arts instructor?
How do I become an astrobiologist?
How much money do language translators make?
How long does it take to become a Web developer?
What are the most interesting areas in the legal field?

And so on.

And then start watching the videos that YouTube serves up for you. They won't all address your exact question, but most of them will be close enough to start telling you things you didn't know to ask. And from there, write down any questions that come to you, and then ask YouTube those questions.

If you don't find any helpful videos, like if your question is too specific, or the field is too obscure, that's ok, just ask Google instead, and you'll almost always find something useful in text form. I only recommend starting with YouTube because video is easier to consume quickly, and it's often of higher quality. There's also just something helpful about hearing people speaking, unscripted, about their profession.

2. Podcasts

Once you've identified a field that you're really interested in learning more about, podcasts are your best friend (well, other than if you happen to know someone who's in that profession).

The reason podcasts are so helpful is because they *immerse you in the culture* of the topic they cover. For instance, if you wanted to become a teacher, you'd find a few podcasts created *by* teachers, *for* teachers. After just a few episodes,

you'll know SO much more about the world of teaching...
and usually, it's stuff you won't hear anywhere else, because
it's the inside "shop talk" between members in that field.
The kind of stuff that would bore non-insiders, so they aren't
as likely to talk about it to people outside of their
profession.

All of this research is meant to help you find something that *sparks
joy* for you. That is, it makes you excited.

It is very important to pursue a career that makes you excited,
because that love for it will make it much easier—or even a total plea-
sure—to power through the hard work that's required.

You want your chosen profession to feel like *your dream job*.

And once you've identified your dream job, think of dreams as, not
just pie-in-the-sky dreams, but as your actual *plans*. When you *plan*
for something, it becomes more grounded and approachable. So look
at all your dreams, and start calling them plans! (This applies to non-
career dreams, too.)

Tip #3 - Go for *Radical Skills Acquisition*

One of the best things you can do for your life is to become a *lifelong
learner*. Which means, not only do you continue learning after you're
done with school, but you actually *love* to learn. It becomes one of
your favorite pastimes. Your hobby. *Your passion!*

Is this you already? If so, *awesome, girl!* Congratulations, you're almost
guaranteed to succeed in life, just by having "learning" as one of your
favorite hobbies. It means that you'll have no problem adapting to
changes, such as new technologies, new techniques in your job, or
maybe even switching careers a few times throughout your life. *You'll
be excited by all of it.*

In fact, lifelong learners start to feel a little bit antsy if they go too long without learning something new. That's a good thing! It motivates you!

If you haven't yet acquired a passion for learning, that's ok, but it's something to work on, by adding lines about it to your Coffee Self-Talk.

If you think about it, learning can be about *anything*. Anything that interests you—hobbies, movies, golf, trivia, world travel, dolphins... whatever—these are all things that you can actively spend time learning more about, and when you're having fun, *it's not work!*

If you learn about fun stuff in your spare time, you'll soon develop the *habit* of liking learning in general. And when that happens, *the world is yours!*

Doing this well involves two things. The first is that you *learn how to learn*. In other words, if you want to know more about something, you want to get good at finding information about it. That can be as simple as going to Amazon.com or the library and looking for books on the topic, or, again, going to Google, or to YouTube and watching videos.

If you want a more structured approach, look into online courses offered by Udemy, Coursera, Udacity, edX, Skillshare, or LinkedIn Learning. Courses range from free, to cheap, to expensive, but the paid courses are usually quite good. Many people currently employed as programmers learned their skills from online courses such as these, without ever studying the subject in college.

The second important thing for becoming a lifelong learner is to focus on having a mindset of *acquiring skills*.

Knowledge is good, and often useful, but *skills* are almost *always* useful.

What's the difference between knowledge and skills?

It's simple:

*A skill is knowing **how** to do something.*

The more things you know how to do, the more resourceful you'll be in your own life, for solving problems and reaching your dreams.

It also means you'll be useful to other people. And that means having economic security... food on your plate and a roof over your head.

Pursuing *radical skills acquisition* is a super badass way to live your life. By "radical," I mean you're like, freakin' nuts about it! You're always super jazzed to learn how to do something new, to get better at it, and maybe even pro-level skills. The harder the thing, the better! Why? Because it's badass, that's why!

It means always learning new skills, whether it's archery, or camping, or Photoshop, or ceramics, or 3D animation, or gardening, or computer security, or Japanese, using a language app like Duolingo. Literally *anything*.

Any time you learn a new skill, you level up! Leveling up in your life means more opportunities. It means more networking potential. More friends. More ways to make money. More ways to entertain yourself and have fun.

More freedom!

If you always have a mindset of loving to acquire new skills, your life will expand in a million incredible ways that you can't even imagine today!

Coffee Self-Talk Script: My Dazzling Future

*I am worthy of a blazing, awesome future. I will make my dreams and plans come true, and it all starts with my mindset: **I Am in Control.***

I am worthy of the most sparkly, shimmery, blissful life.

I have a success mindset, from the moment I open my eyes, to the moment I fall asleep.

I have the magic touch. I go from success to success, and it feels great.

There is no such thing as failure. Setbacks are part of learning, and they always make me smarter, stronger, and more capable.

My future is bright, because I have so many opportunities.

I know how to learn, and I am super resourceful. If I have a question, I dive in to discover the answer, like a treasure hunter digging for gems.

I have fun being myself and going after my dreams, attracting them to me with my abundant positive energy.

I can do anything I put my heart and mind into. It's a great feeling. I say the words, I feel the feelings, and I make it happen.

Success feels good. I feel good. Life feels good. I'm ready for my day, every day.

I stand tall, my face tilted toward the sky. I am powerful, I am epic. I am magic!

Asking for help is easy, and I love helping others, too.

I celebrate all my wins, big or small, because I'm worth it.

Love fuels my positive energy, and every time I need to feel better, I think of something or someone I love.

I have grit, determination, and a growth mindset. I go, and I go, and I go!

I'm a great person. I look on the bright side—it's part of my magical living strategy.

I hold the key to my future kingdom with every word in my mind.

I love life. I love my life. I love me! I am ready for success.

Every day, I get more comfy-cozy in my skin, and my confidence grows.

Acquiring rad new skills expands my life. I love that!

I have a good sense of humor. I'm smart and thoughtful. I am happy.

I have a cool perspective on the world.

My creations are meaningful. My feelings are valued. My self is worthy.

My future success will always have golden doors of opportunities all around, because I attract them with my energy, and my brain knows what to focus on.

Chapter 17

ACADEMIC BADASSERY

Hi, Rockstar!

Want to be an Academic Badass?

If so, this script is for you. It will help you to get better grades more easily, be inspired by your schoolwork, build your confidence in your academic ability, and lay the groundwork for your magical future life!

Question: Why is Academic Badassery important to living a magical life?

Answer: *Freedom and choices!*

Some people like to do well in school to make others happy. Teachers, parents, grandparents, and so on. Or maybe to look smart, or impress people. Or maybe just because they like the challenge. Or because getting good grades makes them feel good.

Don't worry about what others think. Worry about impressing *yourself*, and all the other good stuff will follow. That means living up to *your own vision* of what you're capable of doing. Both creating that vision, and then living up to it, come from your Coffee Self-Talk.

But there's an even bigger reason to do well academically.

When you kick ass in school, you have more choices in life, and this gives you more power and control over your own destiny. It gives you more freedom.

> *Having choices means **you** get to decide what you do.*
> *Other people don't get to choose for you.*

My big life goal as an adult has always been to have FREEDOM! Freedom with my schedule, freedom with how I spend money, freedom with my life. Funny thing, I didn't know that freedom was my "thing" when I was your age. Ironically, I was probably more driven by impressing my mom back then. But I also wanted a great-paying job, because I had... shall we say... *champagne tastes* (hehe).

I still do.

When we were kids, my mom used to drive my brother and me around to different neighborhoods in our city. She'd first take us to a beautiful neighborhood, with perfectly manicured lawns the size of football fields, and driveways the lengths of roads. The houses were spectacular, with all their gleaming windows. As we drove through the neighborhoods, our noses pressed against the glass and looking out of the car, my mom would say, "*This* is what you can have if you study."

Then, she'd drive us to a poor part of town, with trash everywhere, graffiti, homes with shattered windows, and broken-down cars. "And THIS," she would say, "is what you can have if you don't study."

Interesting lesson, Mom. A bit oversimplified maybe, but I have to admit, it stuck in my memory. Mental images of abundant wealth and depressing poverty had much more impact on my young brain than any discussion of grades, jobs, and dollars would have.

However, at the time, even though I knew I wanted success, I had no concept of how that could happen for me, other than the traditional *doctor or lawyer* path. I didn't know there were a million options, and that I should expose myself to as many of them as possible. I never dove into my passions to consider what lit me up, expanded my energy, and made me so excited to read about it that it never felt like studying or work.

Most of all, I didn't have someone teaching me about self-talk.

So, because I didn't know what I wanted, and because I didn't really know myself very well, I ended up trying a few different majors in college. And while I don't think you need to know exactly what you want to be "when you grow up," right now, you can think about the kind of life you want to live, and, from there, let it inspire your passions and your Academic Badassery. The bottom line is, more choices and greater freedom will come from doing well in high school.

In this section, I'm going to share a few gems to help you with school, grades, exams, and studying for success. So you have more choices in life. So you have more freedom.

Key Point to Remember

Focus on impressing yourself, not others. You have permission to pursue what lights you up and burns a fire in your soul.

Self-Talking Your Way Into Academic Badassery

Are you ready to boost your self-esteem and strengthen your grit and resolve? Are you ready to tap into a growth mindset that expands everything in your academic life? Are you ready to take exams with confidence? Are you ready to *enjoy* giving class presentations?

Good. Because all that can happen.

All of your rockstar academic success is going to stem from your Coffee Self-Talk.

Using this superpower is going to help you get better grades, because you'll know that you're smart, brilliant, creative, capable, excited, and loving life. And you won't just be saying it, *you'll believe it*. And then, your brain will take action to hook you up. Your brain has your back. *You've* got your back.

Self-talk works. But you have to do it. You have to show up and take action. The Coffee Self-Talk scripts below will help you do this, by helping you:

- Get organized (if you're not already)
- Study intelligently (see *A+ Tips,* below)
- Have a *rockstar, badass, I-can-do-it* attitude
- Ask questions when you need help
- Make good choices that support your academic focus (Netflix or study? You know what I mean here.)

But here's the thing. Staying focused won't be a hard choice because —*again!*—your Coffee Self-Talk, the little, powerful, 5-minute ritual every morning primes you to WANT to live this way, and to WANT to make the good choices. It isn't hard. You don't have to keep working at it. It actually becomes easy. Automatic.

The new you.

Let's go!

A+ Study Tips

Here are some tips to give you an edge when it comes to studying and Academic Badassery.

Study Tip #1 - Use a Super Study Script

At the end of this chapter, I provide you with a *general* Academic Badassery script. But before we get to that, here's a little mini-script to read through before each study session. Feel free to add any lines that spark excitement.

I am a great student, and studying is easy for me.

My brain is incredible, and I remember everything.

I am fascinated by (name of subject), and I love to learn about it.

(Remember, it doesn't matter if you believe it yet, just say the words, and see what happens. Dislike math? Insert "math" as the subject, and watch what happens over time when you read this repeatedly.)

I am pumped up, focused, and happy. I prime my brain with positive studying energy.

I'm relaxed taking tests, and I get good grades.

I always walk away from the test feeling awesome, my shoulders back, and my head held high.

When I study, I get A, after A, after A.

Study Tip #2 - Focus on Happiness First

It's natural to assume that good grades will bring happiness. I mean, straight A's on a report card is cause for celebration, right?

What is less obvious is that the reverse is also true!

It turns out that happiness is a *predictor of academic success*. When you're happy, such as while you study or sit in class, your happy emotional state actually improves your ability to learn.

That's because positive brains have more resources and energy. Which means your brain is better at learning than on days when you're neutral or sad.

So, while it's important to use words about studying and grades in your Coffee Self-Talk, be sure to include lines about your happiness. (See the script at the end of this chapter for an example.)

Study Tip #3 - The "Just Five Minutes" Rule

Some days, you might not feel like studying. Maybe you had an off day, or maybe you're tired. Whatever the reason, set a timer for five minutes and say, "I'll study for only five minutes." Or "I'll read for just five minutes."

Easy, right?

This baby goal feels good, and it feels effortless because it's only for five minutes. You've turned "studying" into something easy.

The funny thing is, after five minutes, there's a good chance that you won't mind studying longer. Because now you're in *study mode*. In fact, it requires less energy to continue studying than to get up and do something else!

It's kind of a trick you can play on your brain. That's ok. So is self-talk! You're in charge, and you get to use whatever tricks you want to get your brain to do its job and deliver you an awesome, happy life. And along the way, a bunch of A's on your report card!

Pro-tip: This five-minute rule works for all kinds of things: exercising, cleaning your room, and many other tasks that you're having a hard time starting. By making such a tiny goal of five minutes, you *just do it*. Here's a similar trick: "*Bleh... I don't feel like going for a run. So I won't. I'll just sit down here and... put on my running shoes.*" And then guess what happens after your shoes are laced up? I think you know what happens!

Study Tip #4 - Your Daily Rhythm

One of the best things you can do is figure out what time of day works best for you when it comes to studying. For me, I was most effective when I studied in the morning before school and before going to bed at night. I found that, during the day (during and after school), I was distracted, and sometimes I got tired around 4:00 pm. But with a 20-

minute nap, I'd get a second wind, which was perfect to get in some good studying before bed. And there's research to suggest that things we study right before bed get encoded into long-term memory while we sleep. Great!

When you find the best time to do things for your body, you'll find that you can optimize your schedule instead of struggling or trying to force something that doesn't fit you well. For most people, morning and early evening are times when energy levels are higher. Experiment with your schedule, and see where your studying sweet spot is.

Study Tip #5 - Prioritize Sleep

And speaking of sleep and memory, getting deep, restful sleep—*and enough of it!*—is super important for helping you remember what you studied. So get your ZZZ's! Did you know that sleep also boosts creativity? The idea for the Periodic Table of the elements came to scientist, Dmitri Mendeleev, *in his sleep!* I could go on and on about the science behind good sleep for learning, memory, and creativity, but I'll save you the time and just smile sweetly at you while I yell, *"JUST FRIGGIN' DO IT!"*

Study Tip #6 - The Power of Place

Another tip for achieving A+ studying is to take advantage of the *Power of Place.* What does this mean? It's thinking about where you are and what/who you're surrounded by when you're studying.

When you consider where you study, ask yourself, *"Does this environment inspire me?"* Maybe it's the library, or maybe it's a special couch in a groovy cafe, where the tables are filled with other students or successful businesspeople, clicking away on their laptops, getting things done.

When I was growing up, my mom used to drive me *45 minutes away*, to the University of Michigan's library in Ann Arbor, so I could study and work on my projects in a collegiate atmosphere, which felt almost mystical to me at that age. I would feel the energy of the cool, older, disciplined students studying, and I fed off that energy. It inspired me. I wanted to be like them!

And one day, about six years later, *I was one of them!*

(Thanks, Mom!)

Study Tip #7 - Choose Your Friends Wisely

And now for our final study tip:

> *Be mindful of how much time you spend around which people.*

While it's fine to have friends of all kinds—different backgrounds, personalities, and goals—it's also important to remember the saying,

> *You become the average of the five people you spend the most time with.*

That may either delight you or horrify you, depending on who your five people are, haha!

Some of your five might be family members, but the rest are probably your friends. If you have great friends who are ambitious and supportive of your goals (or share them), then that's great. But if they're lazy, or they're not studious, or intellectually curious, or if they have unhealthy habits, well...

Let's just say that, statistically, you're more likely to mimic these behaviors the more time you spend with them, versus friends whose behaviors and attitudes are aligned with those that will help you achieve Academic Badassery and an awesome, magical life.

Studying—and other activities that benefit from discipline, such as exercise, and work—can be massively easier and *waaay* more fun if you're doing it with somebody else who's also serious about it. You end up boosting each other's confidence and motivating one another.

And, you know, actually just having straight-up good times together.

Or you might just be someone who prefers to study alone. And if that's the case, that's perfectly fine, but still be aware of the mindset of the people you spend time around, and choose those people wisely.

Storytime! My husband attended Arizona State University for undergrad, which had a reputation as a "Top-Ten Party School." He was a serious student, but the school's culture made the lure of having, shall we say, *excessive fun*, a constant distraction. He studied hard and did very well, but during the first two years, the constant invitations to party and socialize were like a gravitational pull that he always had to resist. He would decline most invitations, and catch grief about it from his friends. They meant well, but it wasn't a good influence.

In contrast, years later, he attended graduate school at the University of Pennsylvania, an Ivy League school on the East Coast. The culture there was completely the opposite... all of the students were *extreme* Academic Badasses. Although my husband was in his mid-twenties by then, he did take a few graduate classes that were also open to undergraduate students, so he had a few classmates that were the younger age he'd been when he attended the party school, Arizona State.

The difference was night-and-day. The Penn "kids," as he called them, worked harder even than the graduate students. They were driven, motivated, perhaps even to unhealthy extremes. But most notably, it was *the norm for their social existence.* Anybody who didn't study hard would have been shunned by their peers. Considered not only a distraction, but a *loser.* Sure, the Penn kids still partied, but much less, and only after the studying was done. Partying was never a distraction; it was a reward.

And if you really are the average of the five people you spend the most time with, imagine living with a bunch of housemates at one of the two schools mentioned above. (This is not meant to trash talk Arizona State. It's a fine research university, and it's possible to get an excellent education there, but as one professor told my husband, "You just don't have to, to graduate.")

This is not to say that, if you go to university, it must be some elite, Ivy League school. But if you go someplace that isn't, try to seek out the students that *could have* gone to one, and hang out with them. You'll literally become smarter just by hanging out around people who themselves are smart, and working every day at getting smarter.

This applies while you're in high school, too.

Ok! Enough preaching. Now for the fun stuff...

Coffee Self-Talk Script: Academic Badassery

I am worthy of awesome grades. I am an academic badass! Yeah, baby!

I am an incredible creator, I am talented, and I accomplish whatever I focus my energy on.

Getting super grades is fun, and it gives me freedom, power, and choices.

My life gets better each day, because I love myself.

I love being me, and I have fun studying and learning. I'm awesome at studying.

I have a world of opportunities out there for me. I am excited about life!

I can do anything I put my heart and mind into. It's a great feeling. I say the words, I feel the feelings, and I make it happen.

I am creative, full of ideas, and capable. I enjoy a challenge, and I power through them with all of my might.

Anything is possible because I'm unstoppable. I keep on going, no matter what!

School is an opportunity, and I'm taking advantage of it!

I am powerful. My mind is epic.

Science, math, reading, writing, history—the subject doesn't matter. My brain is phenomenal, and easily learns whatever I tell it to learn.

I am a super nice person, and I feel this all day long. I am bright. I sparkle, shimmer, and shine.

I am worthy of excellent grades.

I claim what I want, I believe it's coming, and I'm worthy to receive it. I open my arms and welcome it into my life.

I feel excitement moment by moment, and I have a bright, smiling attitude toward school and studying, because I'm worth it!

I am in charge of my focus, and I choose to see the positive.

I am my own cheerleader. Go, me, go! Here I come, A-grades! I'm doing it!

I'm living a completely new life of my own creative design.

I am full of glittering happiness. My energy and effort bring excellent grades into my life, because I feel good thoughts, and I show up to take action. It's a dance with life. I do my part, and it does its part.

I am confident, and I shine like a star. I am thankful for my life.

Presentations are so super easy to give. I love standing in front of people and sharing my work. I get a rush from it!

My confidence builds and builds. I love my life. I am ready for amazing grades.

I take care of myself by focusing my mind, because I'm worth it. I'm so very, very worth it.

I love helping others. Yes! It feels amazing!

I like learning new things because it's fun. It gives me choices, and it enriches my life.

I can achieve because I'm capable, focused, and I rock!

Chapter 18

RELATIONSHIPS

I have a lot to say about relationships, whether that's your friends, your family, or romance. But I'll boil it down into a few key points.

The Short Version

You want to be around people who uplift you. People who bring out the best in you. People *who make you feel even better about yourself, who magnify the brilliance you're already shining.* People who value you, and your perspective and choices. People who don't pressure you to be someone you're not, unless it's to up your game.

You want to be with people who *feeeeeel* good to be around!

Friends & Peers

Recall what I said in the previous chapter, that *you become like the five people you spend the most time around.* This can be great, or it can be a problem. It happens because of "mirror neurons" in the brain. These special mirror neurons fire and wire pathways in the brain, based on what you *see others doing.* It's how babies learn to speak. It's why laughter is contagious. And yawning. And even vomiting. Mirror neurons can fire from watching people on television, too. You can even start to mirror the people you spend the most time watching on social media. Crazy, huh?

Doesn't this make you want to take a second look at *which* people you allow to be in your life? You have a huge opportunity here. You might want to make some changes. If your friends often elevate your emotions, that's fantastic... hang on to them! Be a good friend back, and be sure to help elevate *their* emotions.

But if your friends aren't amazing, then change your energy, get your butt out there, and make new ones.

I'm sure you've heard about peer pressure a million times, right? But hear me out! I'm going to tell you something you probably haven't heard before, the truth about peer pressure. The adult version...

And that is, sometimes peer pressure is *good*.

What?

That's right. Good. Peer pressure is good when your peers pressure you to live your best life. When they pressure you to strive for your goals. When they push you to get back up when something knocks you on your ass. Good friends are an enormous asset! They can help you create your magical life faster.

Bad friends do the opposite.

They bring you down. Keep you from reaching your goals. When adults harp on about "peer pressure," they're talking about these kinds of people, who pressure you to do things that will harm you or slow down your progress.

Fortunately, there are people out there *right now*, waiting for you, wanting and hoping to connect with you and be friends with you. People who want the best for you, and vice versa. And guess where this all starts? *It starts with you.* Once you level up, and start living your magical life of high-vibing goodness, you'll quickly know who you want to spend time with and who you don't. It will become very obvious when certain people drain your high-vibe energy... you won't like the feeling. Where you never noticed it before, or you tolerated it, you'll now feel the urge to back away from it. Like poison.

When it comes to peer pressure, always remember to look inside yourself for answers. Follow your intuition. It will guide you. Your friends don't know how hungry you are or what you should wear. *You do.* So if everyone else is skipping lunch and you're hungry, then eat! If everyone is wearing tiny, tight clothes and you like baggy... then go baggy. Be your own person. Do whatever is going to fuel your happy vibe.

Dance your own dance!

Also, be the friend to others that you want your friends to be to you. We teach people how to treat us. Again, it starts with you. If you want friendly people in your life, and uplifting interactions with friends, then you need to be friendly and uplifting, too. If you want your friends to have your back, it goes both ways. And I'll tell you... good friends respect and support each other. They don't pressure, they don't boss, and they don't ever make you feel bad. They're never jealous when good things happen to you. It makes them happy to see you succeed. They want you to do well!

Don't be yanked around by the whims of other people. There's freedom in not needing everyone to like you. And it's definitely ok, and even kinda cool, if not everyone understands you.

Thriving Around Negative People

Living the *Coffee Self-Talk Life* changes you, but that doesn't mean it changes everyone around you. Sure, you'll now be able to respond better to negative people... people who aren't drinking the Coffee Self-Talk Kool-Aid with you. But let's be honest, there are still people and situations that warrant almost heroic, Mother-Teresa-like patience to deal with. Well, I have a way to help you manage difficult and negative people.

There are going to be times when you're in the company of people who don't share your enthusiasm for life. Or for amazing words and uplifted emotions. You have some control over how much time you spend with these people, especially the ones you don't live with. People familiar with self-talk know how important it is to surround themselves with other positive self-talkers. It enhances our energy, life experience, and it feels good. We build each other up. If you have a group of friends like this, then huddle up and hug. That's great.

Sometimes, you start to realize that negative people just aren't your jam anymore. You're out of sync with them. You have different visions of what's possible. Like a snake shedding its old, crusty skin, sometimes you have to let go and move on.

Does this mean abandoning people you love? Cutting them out of your life completely? Not necessarily, especially not family. And some people can use your help. Maybe you can show them how to uplift themselves, by teaching them what you have learned. But be careful. Not everyone wants to change, and it's not your job to fix them. Not everyone wants to be helped.

And most of all, before you can help other people, you must always make sure you're getting what you need for your own growth and well-being. If a negative person is going to remain in your life, your self-worth and positivity must be strong enough to not be brought down by their negativity.

Again, being thoughtful about *how much time* you spend with whom is one of the most important habits you can adopt in your entire life. You must be mindful of *external* sources of negative programming, just as you monitor what you're saying to yourself.

And despite your best efforts, there will still be times when you find yourself around Negative Nellies. Perhaps a family member, for instance. Although you might be able to reduce the time spent with that person, it might not be possible to avoid them completely, and honestly, you love them and don't *want* to avoid them completely. Fortunately, there's a clever trick for that!

Whenever I'm around people who are complaining or whining about something, I respond with *"Wouldn't it be awesome if..."* and I completely change the tone of the conversation. For example, if someone complains about traffic while we're in the same car, I respond with, *"Wouldn't it be amaze-balls if we had a car that could lift up, and we could fly over all these other cars?"*

By combining fun words like *amaze-balls* and using a silly scenario, like flying cars, I lighten the mood for myself and others. I don't care where the conversation goes from there, so long as it's not about the traffic. I'm really just trying to disrupt the other person's pattern, to distract them long enough to change their emotional state to something less negative.

If flying cars doesn't do the trick, I might hit them with a random question about something I know they love. "Played any golf lately?" And wow, it's amazing how they sometimes just light up and forget all about the thing that was bugging them.

In some situations, fun words and silliness aren't appropriate. So, for instance, if someone is venting or complaining about their boss, I first listen carefully, as all good listeners do. I don't diminish or dismiss their feelings or experience. But then, I shift the mood and give them an opportunity to think about something else, something better. Such as, *"Wouldn't it be cool if you had your own company doing _____?"* Or *"Wouldn't it be awesome if your boss was super generous and gave you high fives for all the great work you do?"*

So, you want to be sensitive to the situation and respond accordingly, but that doesn't mean sitting there, stewing in their negativity with them. Beyond acknowledging their feelings and showing your sympathy, any additional "Yeah, that really sucks"-talk is only digging them deeper into their emotional hole. You can throw them a rope here, and help pull them out, just by shifting their focus, or in some cases, helping them brainstorm possible solutions. (Keeping in mind that people aren't always asking for solutions. Sometimes they just need to vent.)

And sometimes, when you're stuck with a negative person, you just need to put in some earbuds or go to another spot in the house. It's up to you what programming you let enter your brain, and if you're getting an earful that you'd rather not let dampen your shiny, golden vibe, then just excuse yourself, and go do your own thing. Such as making a cup of coffee and refilling your tank with some awesome Coffee Self-Talk!

Be careful not to judge negative people. They're usually just victims of negative programming, from who-knows-where.

And, even if they direct their negativity directly at you, it often has nothing to do with you. People behave based on how they feel inside. When they feel crappy, or sad, or mad, or lack self-worth, they often project that pain outward into the world, like an injured dog who bites the person who's trying to help it. Try to have compassion for people who are suffering, and don't take it personally. Whenever you meet someone who's negative about *everything*—life in general—it's always because of something going on inside of them. It's not about you.

My parents divorced when I was very young. For many years, there was no dad in my life. This bothered me when I was growing up. It confused me. I questioned why my dad didn't love me enough to get to know me.

But, years later, as an adult, I heard the famous personal development speaker, Tony Robbins, say that people are *just trying to figure out their own lives*. And when they behave in ways that don't line up with my own needs or desires, even if it's a parent, it's not worth worrying about, or letting it impact my beautiful self-worth, because the parent's issues have nothing to do with me. They're not perfect, they have problems just like everybody else, and their behavior is them just trying to get their own life together, trying to figure stuff out. And if they go down a path that doesn't fit with how I'd like things to be, it's not because of me.

When I realized this, and I thought about my dad, I felt compassion for him. And at the same time, my own self-worth began to rise up and grow, because the truth of this idea resonated deep in my soul.

I love the following quote from a hilarious deck of affirmation cards called *AFFIRMATORS!*...

> *"If someone starts to speak unkindly to me,*
> *I'll remember that they've got something*
> *going on that has nothing to do with me.*
> *Like maybe they just pooped their pants.*
> *Yes, that's probably it."*

Romance

When I look back on my life—before I met my amazing husband—I didn't have the self-talk or self-worth I have now. Once I started to have better energy, I started to attract better people into my life. When I started loving myself, and seeing myself as *worthy* of the best relationships, that's when I started having the best relationships.

Here's the bottom line with romantic relationships:

Attracting good people into your life starts with working on yourself.

When you like who you are, two things happen...

First, you get comfortable in your own skin. You like spending time alone, and with family and friends. You may prefer to be in a romantic relationship, and perhaps actively seek one out, but importantly:

Your happiness does not depend on being in a relationship.

Second, when you like who you are, remember that you start sending out your shimmery-shiny confidence vibe into the world, *without even trying.*

As I've mentioned before, *people notice!*

It's very attractive. Literally... it *attracts* people.

It's attractive to all kinds of people, but especially those with confidence and high self-esteem of their own. It's like the old saying, *birds of a feather flock together.*

But something else also happens. You become more *selective.* Partly because your boosted self-esteem seeks similar traits in a romantic partner. But also because you have more options, because more people are noticing you. Or responding positively if you approach them.

Suppose two people are interested in you. One of them has good energy, the other has bad. Which one are you going to choose? Who would you rather be with? When your energy is good, you're going to feel much more comfortable and excited around the individual with energy that matches your own.

But that's just the beginning of the story...

Once you're in a relationship (if you choose to be in one), your high self-esteem helps ensure that you're only in a *healthy* relationship.

You will require courtesy and respect from your partner. Anybody who does not treat you well will not meet your standards. And because your self-esteem is strong, you will be fine parting ways, if necessary.

One last bit on the romance front...

Always remember that:

You are in charge of your body.

When you make decisions that honor your truth, and respect your desires—that is, the things that feel good in your heart—you'll soar like an eagle.

As a teenage girl, I found myself in situations where guys were real gentlemen... and I've been in situations where I felt pressured. In the times I felt pressured, I can really only describe it as feeling very lost, even scared, because I didn't know what to do or say.

I have two tips for you here...

1) Once you've built up your self-worth, it becomes very clear what to say, do, not say, and not do in these situations. You quickly weigh the pros and cons of different choices in the moment, and you feel good about whatever you choose, because you've been true to yourself, and the things that are important to you.

> *When you honor yourself, you feel confidence. Grace.*
> *When you feel lost or frightened, something is wrong.*

But if you're still working on your self-love and self-worth, if you're still building your self-confidence, and you find yourself in a sticky situation where you don't know what to do, here's my next tip:

2) Be prepared! The trick is to come up with two or three lines ahead of time, things you can say that will buy time while you figure out your next move. Think of those lines now, like blaming it on parents, or allergies, or needing to go study for a test, or just simply not being ready to do something, or simply say that you're leaving.

When you have these lines ready to go, you'll deliver them confidently, without hesitation, in a tone that conveys your decision is final, not open to negotiation. That alone tends to end the conversation. My personal favorite is to simply say, with real sass and a self-empowered attitude, *"Awww, hell no, I'm not doing that."*

Coffee Self-Talk Script: Attracting Awesome People Into Your Life

I attract the most amazing relationships, and they match my amazing energy.

I am love. I am friendly. I love my relationships.

I am a great daughter.

I am a great sister. (If you have a sibling.)

Happiness is around me and inside me, and it attracts magical people into my life.

Rainbows are all around. I run up them and slide down them, hands in the air, free to just be me.

I believe in me. I open my heart, and I'm true to myself. When I do this, I allow others to be true to themselves, too.

I'm a glittering rainbow unicorn, and I wear this badge with shimmer-shine pride!

I love my relationships, and they love me.

I dance my dance, loose and fun. I'm spirited, I'm brave, a moonshot of momentum.

I love my friends, and they love me.

I have the best friends in the world. We love each other, and we make each other stronger.

When I'm confident, people have confidence in me. It's time to be awesome.

People trust me, and I am worthy of their trust.

Time with my friends is precious. We have the best time together!

I feel unlimited generosity and patience with myself and others.

My friends and I have each other's backs, and we are always there for each other, no matter what.

I am excited to see my friends and family. My community rocks.

I am filled with love, and I welcome the most amazing friendships into my life.

My dreams are coming true as I speak these words. I say it, I feel it, and I'm open to receive it.

I trust my friends, and they trust me. Our time together is filled with laughter, fun, and exciting adventures.

I am safe with my friends, and they are safe with me.

My world is expanding with brightness, and it shines everywhere. I am worthy of everything I desire.

I attract fun friends with big hearts, and we love doing new things together.

I'm receiving everything in the dream life I design, because I'm worthy.

I'm powerful and capable of doing anything I want. I go after it!

My color shines and lights up my life and the lives of others.

Chapter 19

BEAUTY & BODY

When you say uplifting, positive self-talk such as,

I am pretty, I have a healthy body, I love my body,

... you actually start to think this, and really feel it.

If you currently don't think these things, then I promise, when you simply start saying them as part of your daily Coffee Self-Talk, they'll fire and wire, and you will start to feel them over time.

With your own Coffee Self-Talk, feel free to be specific about physical traits that you'd like to promote. For instance, having beautiful, clear, glowing skin, lustrous hair, and a fit body. (Self-talk won't change your genes, but it can affect your genes' expression, your hormones, and, of course, your behavior.)

If you're into sports or fitness, then this is the place where you could talk about improving your squat or your bench press. Or motivating yourself to work out more consistently. Remember...

You can use your self-talk for anything.

For example, you might have a line that says,

When I wake up every morning, I jump out of bed and do 20 push-ups.

Or,

I love doing jumping jacks.

Or,

I take a 20-minute walk every other day.

Or,

I have gorgeous, clear skin.

Even if your skin isn't clear right now, remember, you still want to say it *as though the future has already happened.* That is, you want to describe to your brain the *you that you're becoming.*

The more you say these things, the more laser-focused your brain will be at making it become a reality.

Super Important!

It's super important that you love yourself, and your body, and your hair, and your face, and every part of you... *right now.*

Love yourself as you are now, and you'll automatically *start to see* changes. This is critical. If you don't love yourself as you are now, you won't feel worthy enough to improve. Don't wait to love yourself later, after the changes have happened. Because if you don't love yourself, you might subconsciously sabotage your progress.

If you find yourself having a hard time loving yourself now, then go back to Chapter 15 (Self-Love) and focus on that first. Use the self-love Coffee Self-Talk script provided in that chapter to get yourself into an awesome, sparkling, self-loving headspace. Or feel free to combine it with the script in this chapter on beauty, below.

Pro-tip: Be super mindful of what you let into your mind—at all times, really—but especially when you are on social media. Remember, most people are posting their very best pictures and they are *filtered like crazy*. They are *not* reality. Don't get stuck in a nasty loop of comparisonitis. You are beautiful today, tomorrow, and forever.

Do you hear me?

You are beautiful, girl!

How do I know without seeing you? Because *every girl is beautiful*, and when they find their heart, and unleash it with uplifted emotion, and let it *sing and dance*, then there's nothing that can stop that beauty from beaming out.

And let me tell you... *everybody you meet will notice it!*

A Word About Diets

I used to call myself a "serial" dieter. Meaning I would do one diet, then another, and another.

I was 19 years old. I got into bodybuilding, and the habit of working out and eating "healthy" stuck with me. Since then, I've experimented with *many* diets. I even had a whole career writing books about some of them!

On one of these diets, I ate my entire day's worth of carbs in a 60-minute window. In another diet, I was a vegan (no animal products) for 10 years. Some of those years, I only ate uncooked vegan food. Another time, I went carnivore and *only ate meat* for a couple of years! And there was the time I did a strict Paleo diet (foods that were available to our hunter-gatherer ancestors). And another one where I made my own organic sourdough bread and only ate "whole foods."

You get the picture. Lots of experimenting and diets. Some of them pretty extreme.

Were any of them better than the others? Perhaps, but in the end, you know what I really learned?

Thinking about my diet so much
stressed me out more than anything else.

Over time, it only got more and more stressful. And... funny thing, the bottom line to health is *not to be stressed*. Stress creates chemicals in your body that do real damage over time.

If you're following a particular diet, and it stresses you out, then that diet is not helping you. The diet might be ok, but you've got to approach things with a healthy mental attitude, and I had not yet learned how to do that. *I was a bit of a mess!*

The other thing to know is that not everybody is the same.

We all have different genes, and some people respond differently to different diets. While we all have certain, basic nutritional needs, we metabolize things differently in some cases. So I encourage you to explore what to eat based on your own body, and your own desires and goals. Get the fundamental nutrients, and your future self will thank you. To find out, don't be afraid to explore, learn more about nutrition, and try different things.

The truth is, though, when you consistently come back to your brain and your self-talk, your *words and thoughts* play an enormous role in making you healthy, beautiful, fit, and athletic. When you focus on getting your words and thoughts right, you'll always set yourself up for success. You'll always make it easier to attain your goals. Your brain controls so much of what's happening in your body. In fact, your brain can literally *change your body*. This means *self-talk* can change your body, too!

It's not magic though, it's science. It's just how the brain works, controlling everything else in the body using a complex system of hormones and other chemical signals that affect everything from your metabolism, to losing weight, to muscle growth, to your genes... and even how fast you heal from injury and sickness!

Did you know there's research showing that *what you think about* can change your physical body without you actually doing anything physical? That's how powerful our minds are. They've done studies where people *imagine* themselves flexing a muscle, and they achieve *actual physical strength gains*—without having lifted a finger! *Like—um, wtf?* Mind blown! Who needs a gym when you can just tap into the Matrix of your mind and get buff? Hehe.

But seriously, the subjects in this study were activating pathways in their brains related to movement, so those parts of their brains thought they were physically moving, even though they weren't.

When the researchers hooked up the people to MRIs to image what was happening inside the brain, the imaging depicted the same brain activities that happen when the muscles are actually lifting real weights.

Isn't that crazy? It's just like when you're drifting off to sleep, and you dream that you take a misstep, and your whole body jolts in bed. Have you ever had that happen? The brain thinks it's real!

That's the kind of power we all wield with our very own minds. If you give your brain the right instructions, it will go to work, helping to make it happen for you.

And how do you give your brain the right instructions?

I'll bet you know the answer to that by now. <wink>

Coffee Self-Talk Script: I Am Beautiful, Inside and Outside

I am BEAUTIFUL!

I am lovely, inside and out.

I love my life, and it shows in my beautiful smile. My smile is so great, that it's like sparkling stars. I should be in a toothpaste commercial. :)

I love taking care of myself and my body.

I have fun playing, laughing, and being myself. I like me.

I focus my mind on feeling beautiful and strong, and that's what happens. I feel beautiful and strong.

I have a healthy body, and I love moving it, every chance I get.

It's fun playing sports and doing activities outside with other people. I look for opportunities to do this.

I am beautiful. We are all beautiful!

I am worthy. We are all worthy.

I am the best me.

I am a good person. I sparkle, shimmer, and shine. I am bright and confident.

I am worthy of kindness from others. We all are.

I love and accept myself as I am right now. Here and now.

I love being super active, because it's fun and keeps me in great shape.

My heart is healthy, my brain is powerful. My insides are healthy and beautiful, and this sparkling beauty is reflected on the outside, too.

Life is great because I make it so. I have the power to make my dreams come true.

I'm open to the amazing energy that's all around me and supporting my beautiful dreams.

My skin is pretty, and clean, and clear. My hair feels good in my hands.

I love the way my clothes fit on my healthy body.

I love to dance, walk, and move around. It feeeeels so good.

I am confident, and I shine like a star, because I am thankful for my life.

I like myself, because I'm super likable. I'm kind. I'm fun.

I like taking care of my body, and it always keeps me healthy and strong.

PART V

GETTING YOUR SPARKLE BACK

Even with Coffee Self-Talk in your life, there are sometimes going to be challenges. In this section, I'll tell you some really cool tricks to do whenever you're:

- Feeling sad
- Having anxiety
- Having an OOOF day
- Dealing with a mistake or failure

With these tricks up your sleeve, you'll be back to your magical, sparkling self in no time!

Chapter 20

SADNESS & ANXIETY

If you're depressed, you're living in the past. If you're anxious, you're living in the future. If you're at peace, you're living in the present.

— LAO TZU

The first time I heard this 2500-year-old quote from Lao Tzu, I was listening to a podcast, and I stopped in my tracks right on the sidewalk. *It made so much sense!* It was a lightbulb moment. *Ding-ding!*

I immediately took each line and applied it to my own life, trying it out. Tasting it. And the truth of this wisdom surged through me like an electric current.

When I'm sad, it's because of something that has already happened, but I haven't let go of it yet. *The past.*

When I'm anxious, it's because I'm nervous or scared about something that might happen. *The future.*

And when I'm at peace, I'm not thinking about either of those.

Brilliant!

Feeling Sad

Most of us (all of us?) occasionally have days when we're just not bright and chipper. The sparkle is gone, and instead, we're blue. In a funk. Sad about something that has happened. Or about something a friend said. Or sad about nothing at all. Low energy, don't feel like doing anything, or mildly depressed. (I'm not talking about *clinical* depression, which is a long-term condition that should be treated by a healthcare professional.)

At times like this, your brain is stuck in a loop. You think about something sad or depressing, and then you feel sad or depressed, which makes you think about the thing again, or other sad things, and round-and-round it goes, and you're stuck there, until something breaks the pattern.

Or sometimes it's just hormones... you feel depressed without even thinking about anything sad. I've had days when I felt this way when there was absolutely not one bad thing going on in my life—I even looked hard, and I couldn't think of any—and I still felt crummy! Wtf? And then I realized, oh, right, it's that day of my menstrual cycle. This just sometimes happens to me during that time.

So, what can a girl do when she feels this way?

Fortunately, *I have some answers!*

At times like this, you need to change the pattern of chemicals that are swirling around in your head. You might think there's a way to do this with *thought*—meditation, self-talk, whatever—and that helps, yes, but there's another reliable way when your brain gets stuck in a loop. It's a secret backdoor into this process. A way to short-circuit the chemical loop. A way to directly change the chemicals themselves!

And that is: *movement.*

Physically moving your body changes your brain's focus, which means it *must* start diverting different neurotransmitters (the chemicals I mentioned) to make your muscles work correctly. The more exertion, or the more physical dexterity required, the better. In fact, if you were to suddenly sprint up the side of a mountain, or dive into a swimming pool and swim ten laps, I can virtually guarantee that it would break the spell, and make you start to feel fantastic.

But there's also something milder, something that's *juuust* easy enough, that you might be able to scrape your ass off the couch and do it. And that is...

Go for a walk.

Yes, a walk. Around the block. Nothing intense. No special outfit or shoes required. If you can manage to just take the *first step* out the door, the rest will happen automatically. Without you really thinking about it.

The *motion* of taking steps will begin the chemical process that I mentioned above. Your thought patterns will start to change. Maybe to thoughts of random (but not sad) things. Like, why *do* Fig Newtons stick together? Or maybe you start looking at the things around you... it could be anything... a car passing by, the neighbor dude watering his lawn, a cloud that's catching the sunlight in a cool way.

And during these walks, as you might guess, I also rely on my self-talk. But I'm gentle about it. Low-key. Chill. I pick one short phrase... my favorite is:

I am worthy.

And I repeat it over and over. It really helps. Other good ones are:

I love myself.

And,

I am safe.

When I combine a walk with a gentle attitude of grace from my self-talk, it does wonders toward getting me back on a happier path.

For centuries, certain writers, scientists, and mathematicians have walked every day to clear their minds. Or to take a break from work, and then the solution to some problem they've been struggling with suddenly becomes obvious to them during the walk. Walking—especially when you're alone, and not talking on your phone, etc.—does something cool to our brains, kind of like putting you into a trance. You can take advantage of this little quirk of the human brain to fix yourself when you're not your normal, happy self.

With me, *100% of the time,* it makes me feel at least *a little bit* better. Well enough that I can then do other things that might help, such as distracting myself with an activity, like making dinner, watching a show, writing, etc. And that's really all that's required, just getting the ball rolling, and I'm well on my way to feeling normal.

Walking sometimes even gives me just enough motivation to do some real exercise. Like working out, or doing a set of walking lunges across my living room, or otherwise getting my heart rate up. And then, as with the running-up-the-mountain example, I'm all better. Pretty much back to my normal self.

The point is, don't aim for something big. Or even the whole walk itself. Just the first step. No matter what your mood, you can almost always manage to slip on some shoes and step outside the front door. And from there, the rest will take care of itself.

OOOF Days

Living your magical life doesn't mean you never bump up against issues. Or mean people. Or crappy situations. Those are just part of life.

But you don't need to live in fear or anxiety about them. And you don't have to let them ruin your day. If you choose to, you can just notice them, and let them wash over you like a small wave on a sandy beach, and then you return to your normal, beautiful self.

It's never the thing itself... it's how you react that matters.

When you fire and wire your positive self-talk words into your brain, you can choose words that will train you to react to any situation in life more calmly. It's an amazing life skill.

And sometimes we just have an *OOOF* day. A day when we're tired, or cranky, or hormonal, or overwhelmed, or something happens that just makes you go *OOOF!* Like when you show up for class and remember you left your homework... on the kitchen table. *OOOF!*

And on days like these, it's perfectly fine to just take a timeout.

Pick out your favorite book or your favorite Netflix show to watch. Grab some snacks and a bottle of nail polish and paint your toenails. Get out your journal and draw or write. Listen to relaxing or uplifting music... There are all kinds of ways to get back to feeling great. Part of loving yourself is that you recognize when you could use a little self-love, and then you give it to yourself.

Anxiety

Anxiety is a feeling of worry, fear, or nervousness. It can cause a fast heart rate, sweating, or a tight feeling in the chest. Many teens suffer from anxiety, caused by short-term things like taking a test or public speaking. Or long-term things, like one's looks, body, social acceptance, and conflicts with peers or authority figures. Anxiety can also be caused by changes in hormones associated with puberty.

Let's take a look at this and find a way to shine instead.

Recall this line from the Lao Tsu quote at the beginning of this chapter:

If you're anxious, you're living in the future.

How true! Anxiety and worries come from imagining *negative things in the future*. Things that have *not* happened yet. If you take a moment to ponder any times you've felt anxious in the past, you'll find this to be true.

Fears. Anxiety. They come from *worrying about the future*. BUT! With positive self-talk, you can wash away that anxiety.

How, you ask?

By replacing your anxious thoughts about the future with thoughts and feelings of *love*. Right away, at the moment you feel anxiety creeping in. If you feel anxious, about anything at all, change your thoughts to anything you want that's related to love. Love of your mom, or dad, or dog, or cat, or bookstores, or chocolate, or rain, or a certain song. I repeat, if you feel fear, anxiety, or unease, then flip the switch to love: friends, flowers, springtime, new horizons, possibilities.

And it works!

How?

The brain is *neuroplastic*, baby! It can *change*. If there are things that gave you anxiety in the past, it doesn't always have to be that way. Once you start to rewire your brain for love and happiness, the anxiety wiring starts to weaken. Eventually, it loses its power.

And the more you do this love-replacement trick, the easier it gets, and the more effective the results. Pretty soon, your emotions are unavailable for anxiety because you're filling your beautiful heart with feelings of love and living your legendary life. It's the *new you*. Pure transformation. Like a butterfly!

The thing about anxiety is that the tension, the worried thoughts, the fear... they are all operating from *survival emotions*. All of them feel uncomfortable, but they can all be addressed with love, because there's something fascinating about your brain: *It's basically incapable of feeling those opposing feelings at the same time.*

Use that to your advantage.

Gone are the days of tight shoulders and scrunched-up foreheads. Starting now, you can welcome feelings of relaxation. Because, when you are loving, you cannot be fearing, which means anxiety doesn't have a home. *Buh-bye,* anxiety.

And by the way?

Self-Talk is a well-established cognitive therapy used for treating anxiety. It's totally legit! You could even say it's... *sciency!*

So saddle up, girlfriend! You can train your brain to automatically feel love (or for that matter, any elevated emotion) anytime the world knocks at your door trying to scare you about the future. When this happens, you very simply answer the door with love...

Knock knock.

Who's there?

Anxiety and fear.

Go away, there's only Love here.

This little rhyme might seem silly, and that's the point. Being light-hearted is a step in the right direction. If you can remember this cute riddle, and let it serve as a reminder to always open the door to love, then fewer and fewer things will cause you fear and worry in your life. And after a while, you just respond to everything with love. It's like walking through life feeling light, feeling unencumbered. Feeling bliss.

And what about the future? Will that scary thing happen?

Maybe. Just shrug. *"What happens, happens,"* you say. *"Life will go on."* And you stop thinking about it, because you're too busy thinking about all that stuff you love and adore.

Is this just burying your head in the sand? Avoiding facing your problems? Not at all. I never said you shouldn't *work* at solving your problems. I said you shouldn't *worry* about them. As in, giving them *negative emotional energy*.

Worrying never solved anything.

In fact, worrying is one of your least resourceful states! It can paralyze your ability to solve even simple problems. So, if you want to solve something you're anxious about, the first step is to *stop worrying* about it. Once you've done that (by filling your thoughts with love), then you're in a much better state to either A) work at solving the problem, or B) ignore it if there's nothing you can do about it. And it's amazing how many things people worry about are completely out of their hands.

If you can't affect something,
it doesn't deserve your emotional energy.

Guess what?

I used to live in fear.

I used to fall asleep with fear, and then wake up with fear. It was irrational fear and anxiety, and it was totally unnecessary. What did I fear? Does it really matter? The question is, *why* did I feel fear? I didn't think I was worthy. I felt I didn't deserve to live a fear-free life. The truth is, I didn't even really understand what *self-worth* meant. And it was through my self-talk that I learned about self-love, and through my self-love, I started automatically feeling worthy. And the effect was so intense, that's when I learned how profound self-worth is.

Once I came to value myself, and I realized I was worthy of living without fear, the anxiety in my life just sort of faded away...

Now, if something sketch comes knocking on my door, I have *a tool* for how to respond. I grab my tool of love, or my tool of gratitude. In fact, the door to my mind now has a sign that says, "*No fear allowed.*" And you know what? It hardly ever comes around anymore. That's how self-talk works.

So go boldly forward into your life, full of worthiness and love, because I'm here to tell ya, you are worthy of peace and greatness. You are so very, *very* worthy.

We all are.

Anxiety or Excitement — Which Is It?

It's easy to confuse excitement with anxiety. Weird, huh? It's true. The physical sensations are the same: fast heartbeat, sweating, butterflies, etc. But the *meaning* is different. And the effect on our well-being is *completely* different.

Because they feel similar, it's possible to think we're anxious, when really, it's just a form of excitement. For instance, feeling the jitters when getting ready for a date. But now that you know this, you can train yourself to be aware of the difference.

By the way, caffeine can have the same effect on some people (especially if they have a gene that makes them extra sensitive to caffeine). Caffeine is a stimulant, and just one cup of coffee, or an energy drink, makes these people feel super nervous, like they're about to give an oral presentation. But once they know caffeine makes them feel this way, they can learn to recognize in the moment that it's the caffeine doing it, not something going on around them. They can "compartmentalize" the feeling... that is, they sort of *put it in a box*, so to speak. The racing heat thing is still there, but it no longer feels scary, because they know it's just the caffeine.

In a similar way, you can train yourself to recognize the *physical sensations* of anxiety, and stick them in that same box, where they're no longer scary.

That's a pretty cool trick. But it gets better!

You can trick your brain by telling it that scary things (say, public speaking, for some people) are actually just exciting!

I know it sounds a little weird, but suppose you must give a speech for some class—and it's giving you anxiety—well, you might as well reframe that feeling and tell yourself it's not fear, it's excitement.

How?

With your self-talk, of course!

You'll still feel those jitters, but with practice, the *meaning* will actually start to change in your mind. It actually will *be* exciting. And that's an amazing superpower, to be able to convert scary things into exciting things. It's great for much more than public speaking. Like athletic events. Or dates. Or taking tests. Or job interviews. All of these things, if you think about it, *are* exciting to some people. Self-talk yourself into one of those people!

I did this myself!

I used to get nervous when I was preparing to do a podcast interview or talk in front of a live group of people. The funny thing is, the talks always went great, and I felt awesome afterwards, so I really had nothing to fear. Yet, every time, just before we were about to begin, I felt those crazy, heart-pounding jitters. I didn't like it at all! To the point that I almost considered not doing any more interviews!

But now, I've completely reframed the experience into one of genuine excitement. Like I'm about to step onto a roller coaster... and I *freakin' love* roller coasters! Now, every time I'm about to speak or do an interview, all I feel is excitement. And it fuels me, amps up my energy level, and makes me feel like a rockstar!

If I can convert something as scary as public speaking into something as fun as riding a roller coaster, then anybody can. The techniques will work on anyone, because our brains all work the same way. Coffee Self-Talk, to the rescue!

Coffee Self-Talk Script: Addressing Anxiety

I am resourceful.

I am worthy and brave.

My shoulders are relaxed because I am safe.

My forehead is relaxed, because I am fine, and I am lovely.

I inhale peace with every inhale. I exhale peace with every exhale.

I help myself by thinking positive and calming thoughts. I breathe peace and relaxation. I liberate myself from anxiety and release it. I watch it go, up, up, up, and away from me.

I am loved deeply. I open my hands. I am free.

I live a life driven by curiosity, silly playfulness, and being open to all of life.

I am in charge of my thoughts and actions, and it feels amazing.

I am open to how tomorrow wishes to unfold for me. I choose positivity.

Whatever happens, I'll be just fine. I trust myself to adapt and grow in any new situation.

Calm, soft waves on the shore of my mind soothe my thoughts. I am safe.

I am in the right place, at the right time.

I release the need for approval from others from my life. My mind is relaxed. My body is relaxed. Deep breath.

I am loved deeply, and my uplifting energy spreads to others.

I feel the marvelous magic of letting go of anxiety. My life expands with peace right now. Right here.

I appreciate life... I appreciate love... I appreciate me.

Chapter 21

FABULOUS FAILS

From here on out, if you have a failure, you're going to take a new perspective:

Failure is FABULOUS.
And I'm going to learn from it.

I know what I'm talking about. First of all, I'm very successful. I have the love of my life, a beautiful family, I love the work I do. I mean, I get to travel the world, sip cappuccinos in cute cafes in the sunshine... that's my workday. It's amazing. I'm living a magical life. And I didn't get here by accident. Have I had failures along the way?

Abso-freakin'-lutely!

I didn't get here without some pretty spectacular fails. But, you see, being successful requires that you learn a lot, and keep learning, pretty much for your whole life.

Specifically, learning what works... and what doesn't.

When you learn something that works—it could be anything, from learning to make sourdough bread, to running a business—that's great, count it as a success. But for every successful way to make a loaf of sourdough, or run a business, there are a thousand ways to mess it up! And nobody perfects her art without exploring, and exploring means finding both what works *and what doesn't work.*

We call the things that didn't work "failures," but that's unfortunate, because they're really just learning how *not* to do something. Thomas Edison "discovered" over a *thousand* ways *not* to make a light bulb, and then he hit on the one that worked. He did not give up!

Here's a quote I love:

> *Success comes from making good decisions.*
>
> *Good decisions come from experience.*
>
> *Experience comes from making bad decisions.*
>
> — Tony Robbins (paraphrasing Mark Twain)

My magnificent fails taught me SO much! If you have a failure, then rejoice, and learn from it! Even if it feels crappy in the moment, you'll kick butt the next time.

Why don't we naturally celebrate failure? Why does it feel so crappy?

When you make a mistake or have a failure, your brain sees it as a threat, and instead of squirting those happy chemicals I've mentioned before, your brain tells your glands to squirt a stress hormone called *cortisol.* Cortisol does not feel very nice inside you. Your brain does this to get you to take action and change whatever caused the stress in the first place. These processes were laid down in our brains when failure meant life or death... like, if a cave man threw his only spear at the charging saber-tooth tiger... and missed! *OOOF! Better run!*

So, cortisol means well. Its job is to help you run faster from tigers. That's why it makes your heart pound. But cortisol doesn't understand that, in our modern world, failures rarely involve *actual physical danger*.

So I'm going to tell you how to minimize its effects, get rid of the crappy stressful feeling, and make your fails *FABULOUS*.

The interesting thing about cortisol is that it doesn't last very long in the body. It breaks down, and then you no longer feel crappy. So if you feel stressed or anxious about something, if you change your focus and find something to distract yourself, your body will start to clear out the cortisol. And once this happens, you can approach the situation with a calm, clear mind. You can even laugh at it, or learn from it, and get back to focusing on your goals and your amazing life. If the stress is extra high, you might need to repeat the distraction step, to give your body more time.

Now that you understand *why* you feel icky from a failure, you can just shift your focus to something else you enjoy... Coffee Self-Talk (woohoo!), reading a great novel, playing a video game, lifting weights or walking, dancing, talking with friends about fun stuff, listening to music, cooking, etc. And just ride it out while the cortisol disappears, and the crappy feeling just *fades awaaaaaay*.

Then, once you're relaxed, you're in a better frame of mind to process the situation and figure out how to prevent it from happening again in the future.

So, you learn from it, let go, and move on.

The Brilliant Question

And here's a pro-tip for dealing with fails, problems, anxiety, or anything of the like...

Ask yourself this one, simple, brilliant question:

Will this matter in a year?

Seriously... the next time something happens that upsets you, ask yourself that question. So much of life, everything really, is about perspective. When you take a step back and think about the long term, big-picture stuff, it helps you see today's events differently.

Most of the things that bother us are ultimately just *not important*.

At all.

If you break a jar, lose your purse, get in a minor fender bender, fart in front of someone, have a pimple, or a bad hair day, none of these are going to matter one bit in a year, or probably even in a week.

Even something bigger, like if someone breaks up with you, will have a totally different meaning a year from now. The emotions will be milder, or nonexistent. It will mostly just be a memory, and part of the story of your life.

No door closes without another door opening, and when one chapter ends, another begins. When you ask yourself the *"Will this matter in a year?"* question, it helps you benefit now from the hindsight that you will one day have.

So, whatever happens today that upsets you, once you realize that you're probably not still going to be upset a year from now, why be upset now?

Eating Your Liver: Liking What You Don't Like

> *The secret of everyone who has ever been successful is that they formed the habit of doing things that unsuccessful people don't like to do.*
>
> — Albert E.N. Gray

That quote is powerful and just oozes truth. There's really one basic key to success:

Show up. Do the work.

I'm successful because I show up every day. I sit my ass down at the computer and write, whether I feel like it or not. In fact, one definition of "professional" that I like is:

Someone who does the job well, even when they don't feel like it.

And this quote for professional writers in particular:

Inspiration is for amateurs.

In other words, if you're a professional, you don't wait "to be inspired" to do your job. You just sit down and do it.

Now, I say all of the above with a tone that may sound all badass and harsh, but I'll let you in on a little secret...

I never don't feel like showing up!

Why? Because of my Coffee Self-Talk! I absolutely *love* "showing up." I love working. *I love writing!* That's why I don't need inspiration to get started... because I'm always *overflowing* with inspiration! It's "effortless to put in the effort," if that makes sense.

In short: I like doing it.

It's not hard to do things you like doing.

And that's the secret: Converting things you *don't* like doing, into things you *do* like doing.

You see, there are things you need to do if you're going to be successful and live the life of your dreams. Some of them are not fun, but you need to do them anyway (studying, certain jobs, etc.).

I call it "eating my liver."

I never liked liver growing up—it made me want to gag—but I'm an adult now, and I understand its nutritional value. Did you know that liver is *amazing* for beautiful, glowing skin?

Yeah, so I eat my liver.

I do certain things I don't want to do, because I know they're part of making me a blazing success.

But there's a hack for this!

That's right, there's a trick, a stealthy and cool way to use Coffee Self-Talk to reframe your mind about things you need to do, but that you don't really want to do. (This is one of my *favorite* ways to use self-talk!)

When I discovered how powerful the words we use are in determining how we feel and what we manifest, I experimented one day to see how far I could push things. Could I use self-talk to make me actually like... something I *didn't like?*

Or look forward to doing something I previously didn't want to do?

Even before the words came out of my mouth, I was very skeptical. I didn't think it would work. I mean, come on, take something I totally don't want to do, and simply change some words, and suddenly I'll want to do it? I gave the idea my fiercest stink-eye, but then I thought, *what the hell. Might as well try it and see what happens.*

The first time I tried this technique came one day when I had to pay bills. Which I did not enjoy doing. But this time, I tried something different. I simply said,

"I love paying bills. I'm happy to do it."

And that was it.

I had an honest-to-god, immediate shift in my heart. With those simple words, in that moment, I was literally happier to pay bills. It seemed too good to be true, but *oh man*, I ran with it. I said it repeat-edly, over and over, while paying bills, and it got easier and easier.

By telling myself, *I love paying bills*, my mind listened and created that mental state for me. It was *freakin' magic*.

After that, I started using this trick all the time. I remember laughing when it worked so easily, and I thought, *"Yeah, but will this work for other people, or am I, like, just super weird?"*

But then, a few weeks later, I was reading Gretchen Rubin's book, *The Happiness Project*, and she described doing the *exact same thing*. I almost fell off my chair! Hello, fellow fan-girl!

After that first successful experiment, I started using this trick for everything, and I mean *everything*. If there was something I wasn't stoked about doing, I just told myself that I was totally excited about it. At a minimum, this little mental hack took the sting out of doing it. But most often, I actually started *looking forward* to the activity.

For example, when I need to run an errand, like going to the store, when there are other things I'd rather be doing, I change my thoughts. Now I say, "I love going to the store." And off I go, in a better mindset, skipping instead of dragging my feet.

I also use this technique when cleaning. Especially the oven, which I had always disliked doing. I started telling myself "I love it!" I don't even bother coming up with a reason why, because I believe whatever I tell myself. Since the brain takes orders, and I was telling it I loved something, my brain responded with, *"Sure, why not?"*

This trick works extremely well with exercising, too. So many people don't like working out, and some people, my mom included, routinely describe it with a *four-letter word*—and I don't mean *love*! But when you start saying, *"I love exercise!"* every time you're about to do it, you actually find yourself enjoying it. Holy moly, *it totally works!*

Turns out, the trick works on how you feel about people, too. I have this one relative I don't always resonate with. I started telling myself that I loved her, and—honest-to-goodness—*my energy shifted*, and I began to feel more kindness toward her in my heart. And, I'll be damned, I actually found myself looking forward to spending time with her. And when I did, it was so much more pleasant than before. I suspect she sensed something was different, because she seemed to change her energy toward me, too. I mean, it makes sense, right? If I like her, she's more likely to feel the same way toward me. It's as though my words had been a self-fulfilling prophecy.

Which is exactly the point of self-talk!

I'm still amazed at this technique's simplicity. Maybe I'm just weird, but I challenge anyone to repeatedly say *you like something* that you thought you didn't like, and see if your attitude about it shifts, even just a little. If it does, it's worth it. The technique can be used for things you only mildly dislike—like cleaning the house or doing homework—or for things you *reeeally* don't like doing—like giving a speech in front of a class!

Try it yourself. Think of something you need to do this week that you'd rather not do. Simply say out loud, *"I love doing _____."* See if it doesn't instantly make you feel differently about the task. If it doesn't, or if the effect is small, then say it over and over, 5–10 times. Then enjoy the instant lift you experience about the upcoming project or to-do item on your list.

While this tip doesn't require coffee, it's still a form of self-talk. You can use it in your Coffee Self-Talk by adding the statements to your Coffee Self-Talk script. This way, you repeat the positive thought on a daily basis, making the change permanent.

Almost anything can be seen from different points of view. Not everyone dislikes paying bills... bookkeepers, for instance. Not everyone dislikes public speaking. Some people even enjoy it, like my husband. What most people don't realize, is that:

Liking or disliking something is actually a choice.

You see, it's not the activity itself we dislike, but the way we view it.

How we think about things makes all the difference. What they *mean* to us. By speaking just a few words of self-talk, you can completely change what something *means to you*. Be it an activity, a person, or your beliefs about the world.

And most of all, your beliefs about *you*.

WHAT'S NEXT?

OK, Lovely. You're done. *You finished the book!*

Wow, what a journey we've had together! Thank you for sticking with me all the way to the end.

You now possess the key to the magical kingdom. You know that you are in control of your thoughts, your beliefs, your actions, and your life. And that the key to controlling your thoughts is your self-talk. And that the most fun, awesome, consistent way to do self-talk is with what?... Your daily *Coffee Self-Talk*, of course!

That is really all you need to know. Now, you just need to actually *do the doing.* Maybe you started doing your Coffee Self-Talk awhile back, as you were reading this book. Or maybe you were waiting to finish. If you haven't already started, now is the time.

The rest is up to you. *Go live your magical life!*

Well, actually, wait... this doesn't have to be goodbye.

If you'd like more tips and little bits of daily inspiration, I've written *The Coffee Self-Talk Daily Reader #1*. (It covers 30 days.)

There's also a blank journal that's a companion to the book you're reading now. It's just a blank book with lines—any plain notebook will work—but some people like having a special journal that matches their Coffee Self-Talk book. It's a little more fun and reinforces the daily ritual.

Whether you use that or any notebook, you'll want a dedicated place to, at the very least, write down your Coffee Self-Talk scripts. Beyond that, it's a great place to journal your progress, write your thoughts, experiences, make lists, and plan your glorious, magical future.

If you have any questions along the way, don't hesitate to email me.

In fact, I'd love to hear your story! Things like how you're using your Coffee Self-Talk, and what the results have been.

You can reach me at:

Kristen@KristenHelmstetter.com

You can also find me on Instagram at:

instagram.com/kristen_helmstetter

and

instagram.com/coffeeselftalk

I look forward to hearing from you!

Manufactured by Amazon.ca
Bolton, ON